How to Study the Bible

by Jeff Archer

ONESTONE
BIBLICAL RESOURCES

Published by:
One Stone Press
979 Lovers Lane
Bowling Green, KY 42103

Printed in the United States of America

ISBN: 978-1-941422-49-6

ONE STONE
BIBLICAL RESOURCES

www.onestone.com

Objective of the Class

The Bible is God's word to man. God has graciously revealed Himself in the words of the Bible. He has also revealed who we are, what He has done for us and what He expects of us. Sometimes, however, we read the Bible without really comprehending what is being said. How do we study? How do we move from merely reading through the words to seeing the meaning to our own lives? In this class, we will be examining several principles and aids that will help us.

Each week we will have an assignment. Doing the assignments is very important. The goal of the class is for you to learn how to study yourself.

Please bring a pen or pencil, this note book and your Bible to each class.

Be **diligent** to present yourself
approved to God, a **worker** who
does not need to be ashamed,
rightly dividing the word of truth.

- 2 Timothy 2:15

Table of Contents

Introduction - An Overview

I.   Definition of our method.

   A.   There are a variety of valid ways we can approach Bible study. We can study it from a historical, biographical, topical or other perspective.

   B.   In these lessons we will be using a modified version of the **inductive method**.

      1.   The **inductive** method first observes, then concludes. It moves from the specific to the general. The **deductive** method begins with a general principle or conclusion and then sees if that principle is true in practice. It moves from the general to the specific.

         a.   Stated another way, "Induction is the logic of discovery, while deduction is the logic of proof" (Charles Eberhardt).

      2.   Our emphasis will be on the inductive method.

         a.   It means starting with an open mind, a clean slate and an objective look at the Scriptures before drawing conclusions.

II.   We will look at three main areas.

   A.   **OBSERVATION** - We must discover what the passage says.

Objective:

In this lesson we will define our method of Bible study and overview the general principles we will be using.

1. Before we can move to the application of a passage, we must first understand what was being said.

2. We will examine what type of literature a Bible book contains: historical narrative, biographical/autobiographical, poetic, prophetic, letters, law giving/teaching.

3. We will examine a book in the Bible as a whole and try to see the general outline used by the Holy Spirit to convey His message.

4. We will examine the structure of the text: repetition, progression, climax, contrast, radiation, contrast and interchange.

5. We will talk about marking our Bibles in a way that will help us to organize the message in our minds.

B. **INTERPRETATION** - What does the passage mean?

1. This is not always completely separate from the OBSERVING step.

2. We will examine the main rule - context, context, context.

3. We will look for key words, themes, purpose statements to let the Author lead us to the meaning He intends.

4. We will examine figurative language: simile, metaphor, exaggeration, metonymy, synecdoche, personification, irony, parable, allegory and type/antitype.

5. We will examine basic helps such as cross references, concordances, Bible dictionaries, topical Bibles and commentaries.

C. **APPLICATION** - What does the passage mean to me?

1. We will examine the need to pray for the guidance of God.

2. We will examine how God seeks to change our lives.

   a. By statements, commands, principles which set forth His will.

   b. By approved examples which reflect His will.

   c. By necessarily inferring His will in the text.

3. We will examine the difference between general and specific authority as well as the importance of respecting the silence of the Scriptures.

4. We will examine questions that will help us apply the truths of God to our lives.

    a. How would the original readers have applied this passage?

    b. What belief does God want me to accept or reject?

    c. What attitude does God want me to take on or avoid?

    d. What action does God want me to do or not do?

    e. What promise of God can I claim?

III. **Please read the following story and do the assignment at the end.**

The following is a story of a student's crisis under scientist and teacher, Professor J. Louis Agassiz. It was retyped and slightly edited for length from *Independent Bible Study* pp. 173-178. It originally appeared in *Every Saturday*, XVI (Apr. 4, 1874), 369-370, under the title "In the Laboratory with Agassiz, By a former pupil."

It was more than fifteen years ago that I entered the laboratory of Professor Agassiz, and told him I had enrolled my name in the scientific school as a student of natural history. He asked me a few questions about my object in coming, my antecedents generally, the mode in which I afterward proposed to use the knowledge I might acquire, and finally, whether I wished to study any special branch. To the latter I replied that while I wished to be well grounded in all departments of zoology, I purposed to devote myself specially to insects.

"When do you wish to begin?" he asked.

"Now," I replied.

This seemed to please him, and with an energetic "Very well," he reached from a shelf a huge jar of specimens in yellow alcohol.

"Take this fish," said he, "and look at it; we call it a Haemulon; by and by I will ask what you have seen."

With that he left me...I was conscious of a passing feeling of disappointment, for gazing at a fish did not commend itself to an ardent entomologist.

In ten minutes I had seen all that could be seen in that fish, and started in search of the professor, who had, however, left the museum; and

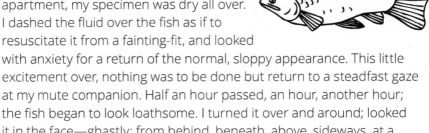

when I returned, after lingering over some of the odd animals stored in the upper apartment, my specimen was dry all over. I dashed the fluid over the fish as if to resuscitate it from a fainting-fit, and looked with anxiety for a return of the normal, sloppy appearance. This little excitement over, nothing was to be done but return to a steadfast gaze at my mute companion. Half an hour passed, an hour, another hour; the fish began to look loathsome. I turned it over and around; looked it in the face—ghastly; from behind, beneath, above, sideways, at a three quarters' view—just as ghastly. I was in despair; at an early hour I concluded that lunch was necessary; so, with infinite relief, the fish was carefully replaced in the jar, and for an hour I was free.

On my return, I learned that Professor Agassiz had been at the museum, but had gone and would not return for several hours. My fellow students were too busy to be disturbed by continued conversation.

Slowly I drew forth that hideous fish, and with a feeling of desperation again looked at it. I might not use a magnifying glass; instruments of all kinds were interdicted. My two hands, my two eyes, and the fish; it seemed a most limited field. I pushed my finger down its throat to feel how sharp its teeth were. I began to count the scales in the different rows until I was convinced that that was nonsense. At last a happy thought struck me—I would draw the fish; and now with surprise I began to discover new features in the creature. Just then the professor returned.

"That is right," said he; "a pencil is one of the best of eyes. I am glad to notice, too, that you keep your specimen wet and your bottle corked."

With these encouraging words he added, "Well, what is it like?"

He listened attentively to my brief rehearsal of the structure of parts whose names were still unknown to me: the fringed gill—arches and movable operculum; the pores of the head, fleshy lips, and lidless eyes; the lateral line, the spinous fin, and forked tail; the compressed and arched body. When I had finished, he waited as if expecting more, and then, with an air of disappointment, "You have not looked very carefully; why," he continued, more earnestly, "you haven't seen one of the most conspicuous features of the animal, which is as plainly before your eyes as the fish itself; look again, look again!" and he left me to my misery.

I was piqued; I was mortified. Still more of that wretched fish! But now I set myself to my task with a will, and discovered one new thing after another, until I saw how just the professor's criticism had been. The afternoon passed quickly, and when towards its close, the professor inquired, "Do you see it yet?"

"No," I replied, "I am certain I do not, but I see how little I saw before."

"That is next best," said he earnestly, "but I won't hear you now; put away your fish and go home; perhaps you will be ready with a better answer in the morning. I will examine you before you look at the fish."

This was disconcerting; not only must I think of my fish all night, studying, without the object before me, what this unknown but most visible feature might be; but also, without reviewing my new discoveries, I must give an exact account of them the next day. I had a bad memory; so I walked home by Charles River in a distracted state, with my two perplexities.

The cordial greeting from the professor the next morning was reassuring; here was a man who seemed to be quite as anxious as I that I should see for myself what he saw.

"Do you perhaps mean," I asked, "that the fish has symmetrical sides with paired organs?"

His thoroughly pleased, "Of course, of course!" repaid the wakeful hours of the previous night.

After he had discoursed most happily and enthusiastically—as he always did—upon the importance of this point, I ventured to ask what I should do next.

"Oh, look at your fish!" he said, and left me again to my own devices. In a little more than an hour he returned and heard my new catalogue.

"That is good, that is good!" he repeated, "but that is not all; go on." And so, for three long days, he placed that fish before my eyes, forbidding me to look at anything else, or to use any artificial aid. "Look, look, look," was the repeated injunction.

This was the best entomological lesson I ever had—a lesson whose influence has extended to the details of every subsequent study; a legacy the professor has left to me, as he has left it to many others, of inestimable value, which we could not buy, with which we cannot part... and to this day, if I attempt a fish, I can draw nothing but Haemulons.

The fourth day, a second fish of the same group was placed beside the first, and I was bidden to point out the resemblances and differences between the two; another and another followed, until the entire family lay before me, and a whole legion of jars covered the table and surrounding shelves...The whole group of Haemulons was thus brought in review; and, whither engaged upon the dissection of the internal organs, the preparation and examination of the bony framework, or the description of the various parts, Agassiz's training in the method of observing facts and their orderly arrangement was ever accompanied by the urgent exhortation not to be content with them.

"Facts are stupid things," he would say, "until brought into connection with some general law."

At the end of eight months, it was almost with reluctance that I left these friends and turned to insects; but what I had gained by this outside experience has been of greater value than years of later investigation in my favorite groups.

In the space below, write down what we can learn about Bible study from this story. (This will serve to overview many of the principles we want to learn in this class.)

_____

_____

_____

_____

_____

In class assignment: Read through Ephesians 2:1-10 - what do you see?

_____

_____

_____

_____

_____

_____

_____

OBSERVATION - WHAT DOES THE BIBLE SAY?

Type of Literature

I.   **Historical Narrative**

A.   Historical narrative is the type of writing in which God simply records historical events for us. He revealed what truly happened in history and selected the events and details He wanted us to understand.

1.   In what way is Genesis an example of this type of writing? _____ _____ _____ _____

2.   In what way is Acts an example of this type of writing? _____ _____ _____ _____

B.   Qualities to keep in mind

1.   All of these events directly or indirectly are connected with God's plan for man's redemption. (This quality is true with every type of writing.)

2.   God does not always state His approval or disapproval of everything recorded.

3.   In the New Testament, things approved by God give us a pattern to follow.

4.   The historical context affects the meaning and application.

Objective:

In this lesson we will be noticing the different types of literature found in the Bible and discussing qualities of each type which need to be kept in mind as we study.

II.   Biography/Autobiography

    A.   This type of writing reports on the life of a particular individual either from his own perspective or someone else's.

        1.   In what way is Esther an example of this type?_____

              _____

              _____

        2.   In what way is Matthew an example? _____

              _____

              _____

    B.   Qualities to keep in mind

        1.   God does not always state His approval or disapproval of everything recorded.

        2.   The historical context affects the meaning and application.

III.   Poetry

    A.   Poetic writing is a style that uses a rhythm of sound or ideas. The use of wise sayings and drama would also fall into this category.

        1.   In what way is Deuteronomy 32-33 an example of this style?

              _____

              _____

              _____

        2.   In what way is Luke 1:46-55, 67-79 an example? _____

              _____

              _____

    B.   Qualities to keep in mind

        1.   Hebrew parallelism

            a.   Psalms 24:1-4—repetition

            b.   Psalms 1:6—contrast

            c.   Proverbs 2:1-5—progression

        2.   Proverbs are truisms, generalities, wise observations—not absolutes.

IV.   Prophecy

    A.   In prophetic literature the author/prophet speaks directly for God. Many times the personal pronoun "I" will be used in reference to God.

1. In what way is Isaiah an example of this type of writing?_____

    _____

    _____

    _____

2. In what way is Matthew 24 an example?_____

    _____

    _____

B. Qualities to keep in mind

1. Some of the prophecies are written in highly symbolic language. It is important to try to understand the point of the symbol rather than try to interpret the symbol literally.

2. Let the text interpret itself as much as possible.

3. The prophecy must first be understood through the eyes of the original readers.

4. Look for keys: Who or what does this prophecy concern? What clues are given within the text for the time of fulfillment?

V. **Letters**

A. Letters were personal correspondence to a particular person or group of people.

1. In what way is Jeremiah 29 an example of this type of writing?

    _____

    _____

    _____

2. In what way is Philemon an example of this type of writing?

    _____

    _____

B. Qualities to keep in mind

1. These were written to a particular person or people. The more you know about the author, the one/ones addressed and the circumstances surrounding the writing, the more accurately you can understand and make application.

VI. **Law Giving/Teaching**

A. All of the Bible could be in this category but there are parts of the Bible where God speaks directly to the people telling them what He wants them to do.

1. In what way is Genesis 2:15-17 an example of this type of writing?_____

_____

_____

2. In what way is Matthew 5-7 an example?_____

_____

_____

B. Qualities to keep in mind

1. Who is speaking and to whom these lessons were spoken.

a. The Law of Moses was given to the Jews, not to all men.

b. The Law of Christ is given to all men but some commands/teaching are to specific people.

OLD TESTAMENT

Genesis _____

Exodus _____

Leviticus _____

Numbers _____

Deuteronomy _____

Joshua _____

Judges _____

Ruth _____

1 Samuel _____

2 Samuel _____

1 Kings _____

2 Kings _____

1 Chronicles _____

2 Chronicles _____

Ezra _____

Nehemiah _____

Esther _____

Job _____

Psalms _____

Proverbs _____

Ecclesiastes _____

Song of Solomon _____

Isaiah _____

Jeremiah _____

Lamentations _____

Ezekiel _____

Daniel _____

Hosea _____

Joel _____

Amos _____

Obadiah _____

Jonah _____

Micah _____

Nahum _____

Habakkuk _____

Zephaniah _____

Haggai _____

Zechariah _____

Malachi _____

Extra Credit

Next to the list of the books of the Bible put what type of literature the book is. Each book will have one main type but may contain portions of other types as well.

NEW TESTAMENT

Matthew _____

Mark _____

Luke _____

John _____

Acts _____

Romans _____

1 Corinthians _____

2 Corinthians _____

Galatians _____

Ephesians _____

Philippians _____

Colossians _____

1 Thessalonians _____

2 Thessalonians _____

1 Timothy _____

2 Timothy _____

Titus _____

Philemon _____

Hebrews _____

James _____

1 Peter _____

2 Peter _____

1 John _____

2 John _____

3 John _____

Jude _____

Revelation _____

OBSERVATION - WHAT DOES THE BIBLE SAY?
Seeing the Whole

Read through lesson 3 first then read the book of 1 Thessalonians following the principles discussed in the lesson. Write down your observations at the end of this lesson and be prepared to discuss your findings in class.

I.   **Step 1**
     Read and re-read the book several times. (If possible, try to read the book through in one sitting. It helps to read aloud.)

   A. Get a feel for the whole. This is important before examining the parts of the book.

       1. Illustration—If you wanted to buy a section of land, what advantage would there be to getting in an airplane and looking at the land from the air?

   B. Don't try to understand every detail of the book at this stage. For now, try to see the overview.

   C. Look for the natural divisions in the book.

       1. Keep in mind that the chapters were arranged either by Stephen Langton, archbishop of Canterbury, in the 13th century. The verses were arranged by Robert Stephens in 1551. These divisions are helpful in finding references but should be forgotten in study when trying to see the organization and progression of thought of the author.

   D. Determine the main message of the book, secondary themes and the relationship these themes have to each other.

Objective:

In this lesson we would like to look at steps in studying a book of the Bible as a whole.

    E.   Observe the obvious.

        1.   Note what type of literature this book is. Note the people that are mentioned. Note the events described. Note the main subjects handled.

II. Step 2

Find as many answers as possible from the text to the 5 "W" and "How" questions.

    A.   Who wrote this book? To whom was it written?

    B.   What does the author reveal about himself and his relationship to the reader? What are key words and phrases?

    C.   When was this book written? What social and/or spiritual situations are indicated in the book?

    D.   Where was the book written? Where is the book sent?

    E.   Why does he write the book? Is there one verse that contains the purpose statement of the book?

    F.   How would the people to whom it was addressed react to this book?

III. Step 3

As you read and re-read the book, write your observations down on a sheet of paper.

Assignment

Write down your observations from your reading of 1 Thessalonians on the next page.

    A.   Write your main observations like:

        1.   The type of literature this book is.

        2.   Summarize the whole book in one sentence.

        3.   Natural divisions.

        4.   A summary of each chapter.

        5.   The key verse of the book.

        6.   Key words and phrases.

        7.   Answers to questions in Step 2.

    B.   (Optional) For future reference, get a folder in which to keep this and all other book summaries.

OBSERVATION - WHAT DOES THE BIBLE SAY?

Introductions

Introductions are written by men to help us understand important background material. They include information such as: internal and external evidence for who wrote the book, the time of writing with historical details that would affect the writing, the purpose, key ideas, survey, outline and other helpful information.

Commentaries and some "study" Bibles contain introductions to each book. Books can also be purchased which contain introductions on each book of Old and/or New Testament.

If you have an introduction for the book of 1 Thessalonians, please read it.

Please also read the introduction taken from *The New Open Study Bible* found in this lesson and answer the following questions.

1. What was the city of Thessalonica like? _____
   _____
   _____
   _____

2. How was the church of Thessalonica established? _____
   _____
   _____
   _____

3. What evidence is there that Paul wrote the book?_____
   _____
   _____
   _____

Objective:

We would like to examine the value of introductions written by men.

4. When did Paul write the book? _____
    _____

5. What keys to the book are mentioned by the author of the introduction?
    _____
    _____
    _____

6. How did the author of the introduction summarize the book?_____
    _____
    _____

7. What other information did you find that will help in understanding the
    book?_____
    _____
    _____

THE FIRST EPISTLE OF PAUL THE APOSTLE TO THE

THESSALONIANS

THE BOOK OF FIRST THESSALONIANS

Paul has many pleasant memories of the days he spent with the infant Thessalonian church. Their faith, hope, love, and perseverance in the face of persecution are exemplary. Paul's labors as a spiritual parent to the fledgling church have been richly rewarded, and his affection is visible in every line of his letter.

Paul encourages them to excel in their new-found faith, to increase in their love for one another, and to rejoice, pray, and give thanks always. He closes his letter with instruction regarding the return of the Lord, whose advent signifies hope and comfort for believers both living and dead.

Because this is the first of Paul's two canonical letters to the church at Thessalonica, it received the title *Pros Thessalonikeis A,* the "First to the Thessalonians."

THE AUTHOR OF FIRST THESSALONIANS

First Thessalonians went unchallenged as a Pauline epistle until the nineteenth century, when radical critics claimed that its dearth of doctrinal content made its authenticity suspect. But this is a weak objection on two counts: (1) the proportion of doctrinal teaching in Paul's epistles varies widely, and (2) 4:13—5:11 is a foundational passage for New Testament eschatology (future events). Paul had quickly grounded the Thessalonians in Christian doctrine, and the only problematic issue when this epistle was written concerned the matter of Christ's return. The external and internal evidence points clearly to Paul.

THE TIME OF FIRST THESSALONIANS

In Paul's time, Thessalonica was the prominent seaport and the capital of the Roman province of Macedonia. This prosperous city was located on the Via Egnatia, the main road from Rome to the East, within sight of Mount Olympus, legendary home of the Greek pantheon. Cassander expanded and strengthened this site around 315 B.C. and renamed it after his wife, the half-sister of Alexander the Great. The Romans conquered Macedonia in 168 B.C. and organized it into a single province twenty-two years later with Thessalonica as the capital city. It became a "free city" under Augustus with its own authority to appoint a governing board of magistrates who were called "politarchs." The strategic location assured Thessalonica of commercial success, and it boasted a population of perhaps 200,000 in the

first century. Thessalonica survives under the shortened name Salonika.

Thessalonica had a sizable Jewish population, and the ethical monotheism of Judaism attracted many Gentiles who had become disenchanted with Greek paganism. These God-fearers quickly responded to Paul's reasoning in the synagogue when he ministered there on his second missionary journey (Acts 17:10). The Jews became jealous of Paul's success and organized a mob to oppose the Christian missionaries. Not finding Paul and Silas, they dragged Jason, Paul and Silas's host, before the politarchs and accused him of harboring traitors of Rome. The politarchs extracted a pledge guaranteeing the departure of Paul and Silas, who left that night for Berea. After a time, the Thessalonian Jews raised an uproar in Berea so that Paul departed for Athens, leaving orders for Silas and Timothy to join him there (Acts 17:11-16). Because of Luke's account in Acts some scholars have reasoned that Paul was in Thessalonica for less than a month ("three Sabbaths," Acts 17:2), but other evidence suggests a longer stay: (1) Paul received two separate offerings from Philippi, 100 miles away, while he was in Thessalonica (Phil. 4:15, 16). (2) According to 1:9 and 2:14-16, most of the Thessalonian converts were Gentiles who came out of idolatry. This would imply an extensive ministry directed to the Gentiles after Paul's initial work with the Jews and gentile God-fearers. (3) Paul worked "night and day" (2:9; 2 Thess. 3:7-9) during his time there. He may have begun to work immediately, but Paul supported himself by tent-making, which took many hours away from his ministry, requiring a longer stay to accomplish the extensive ministry of evangelism and teaching that took place in that city. After Silas and Timothy met Paul in Athens (3:1, 2), he sent Timothy to Thessalonica (Silas also went back to Macedonia, probably Philippi), and his assistants later rejoined him in Corinth (Acts 18:5; cf. 1 Thess. 1:1 where Silas is called Silvanus). There he wrote this epistle in A.D. 51 as his response to Timothy's good report.

THE CHRIST OF FIRST THESSALONIANS

Christ is seen as the believer's hope of salvation both now and at His coming. When He returns, He will deliver (1:10; 5:4-11), reward (1:19), perfect (3:13), resurrect (4:13-18), and sanctify (5:23) all who trust Him.

KEYS TO FIRST THESSALONIANS

Key Word: Holiness in Light of Christ's Return—Throughout this letter is an unmistakable emphasis upon steadfastness in the

1 THESSALONIANS   1412

Lord (3:8) and a continuing growth in faith and love in view of the return of Christ (1:3–10; 2:12–20; 3:10–13; 4:1—5:28). The theme is not only the returning of Christ, but also the life of the believer in every practical relationship, each aspect of which can be transformed and illuminated by the glorious prospect of His eventual return.

Key Verses: First Thessalonians 3:12, 13 and 4:16-18—"And may the Lord make you increase and abound in love to one another and to all, just as we *do* to you, so that He may establish your hearts blameless in holiness before our God and Father at the coming of our Lord Jesus Christ with all His saints" (3:12, 13).

"For the Lord Himself will descend from heaven with a shout, with the voice of an archangel, and with the trumpet of God. And the dead in Christ will rise first. Then we who are alive *and* remain shall be caught up together with them in the clouds to meet the Lord in the air. And thus we shall always be with the Lord. Therefore comfort one another with these words" (4:16-18).

Key Chapter: First Thessalonians 4—Chapter 4 includes the central passage of the epistles on the coming of the Lord when the dead in Christ shall rise first, and those who remain are caught up together with them in the clouds.[1]

SURVEY OF FIRST THESSALONIANS

After Paul's forced separation from the Thessalonians, he grows increasingly concerned about the progress of their faith. His great relief upon hearing Timothy's positive report prompts him to write this warm epistle of commendation, exhortation, and consolation. They are commended for remaining steadfast under afflictions, exhorted to excel still more in their Christian walk, and consoled concerning their loved ones who have died in Christ. The theme of the coming of the Lord recurs throughout this epistle, and 4:13—5:11 is one of the fullest New Testament developments of this crucial truth. The two major sections of First Thessalonians are: Paul's personal reflections of the Thessalonians (1—3) and Paul's instructions for the Thessalonians (4 and 5).

Paul's Personal Reflections on the Thessalonians (1—3): Paul's typical salutation in the first verse combines the customary Greek ("grace") and Hebrew ("peace") greetings of his day and enriches them with Christian content. The opening chapter is a declaration of thanksgiving for the Thessalonians' metamorphosis from heathenism to Christian hope. Faith, love, and hope (1:3) properly characterize the new lives of these believers. In 2:1-16, Paul reviews his brief ministry in Thessalonica and defends his conduct and motives, apparently to answer enemies who are trying to impugn his character and message. He sends Timothy to minister to them and is greatly relieved when Timothy reports the stability of their faith and love (2:17—3:10). Paul therefore closes this historical section with a prayer that their faith may continue to deepen (3:11-13).

Paul's Instructions to the Thessalonians (4 and 5): The apostle deftly moves into a series of exhortations and instructions by encouraging the Thessalonians to continue progressing. He reminds them of his previous teaching on sexual and social matters (4:1-12), since these gentile believers lack the moral upbringing in the Mosaic Law provided in the Jewish community. Now rooted in the Word of God (2:13), the readers must resist the constant pressures of a pagan society.

Paul has taught them about the return of Christ, and they have become distressed over the deaths of some among them. In 4:13-18, Paul comforts them with the assurance that all who die in Christ will be resurrected at His *parousia*

FOCUS	REFLECTIONS ON THE THESSALONIANS			INSTRUCTIONS TO THE THESSALONIANS			
REFERENCE	1:1———— 2:1————		2:17————	4:1————	4:13————	5:1————	5:12——5:28
DIVISION	COMMENDATION FOR GROWTH	FOUNDING OF THE CHURCH	STRENGTHENING OF THE CHURCH	DIRECTION FOR GROWTH	THE DEAD IN CHRIST	THE DAY OF THE LORD	HOLY LIVING
TOPIC	PERSONAL EXPERIENCE			PRACTICAL EXHORTATION			
	LOOKING BACK			LOOKING FORWARD			
LOCATION	WRITTEN IN CORINTH						
TIME	c. A.D. 51						

14 13 1 THESSALONIANS 1

["presence," "coming," or "advent"). The apostle continues his discourse on eschatology by describing the coming day of the Lord (5:1-11). In anticipation of this day, believers are to "watch and be sober" as "sons of light" who are destined for salvation, not wrath. Paul requests the readers to deal with integrity toward one another and to continue growing spiritually (5:12-22). The epistle closes with a wish for their sanctification, three requests, and a benediction (5:23-28).

OUTLINE OF FIRST THESSALONIANS

OBSERVATION - WHAT DOES THE BIBLE SAY?

Marking

You can use your own Bible for this exercise or you can use the copy of 1 Thessalonians provided in the previous lesson.

I. **Marking your Bible** (Suggested marking codes can be found in the table on the back cover)

   A. These marks will help you observe more as you study.

   B. The next time you look at this passage, these marks will help you recall your observations.

   C. Different types of literature will need to be marked differently so it is impossible for your markings to be exactly alike in each book. But try to be as consistent as possible by using a scheme which can also be used in other books.

   D. A pencil and colored pencils work well.

      1. Ink pens tend to run in time and regular highlighters will bleed through.

      2. Highlighters specifically designed for the thin Bible pages also work well but only come in one or two colors.

   E. Try it! Mark 1 Thessalonians.

      1. Write above each chapter or major division your summary statement.

      2. Underline any phrases or sentences that will help you recall the theme of the paragraphs.

      3. By the key verse of the book, write the word "key" or put a "key" symbol.

Objective:

We would like to examine the value of a marking system for our Bibles.

4. Put an asterisk, dot, or star by the main key words and phrases.

5. Put a colored box around each set of verses that fit into the same category.

---

1 Thessalonians 1　　　　　**NEW AMERICAN STANDARD BIBLE**

Thanksgiving for These Believers

[1]Paul and Silvanus and Timothy, To the church of the Thessalonians in God the Father and the Lord Jesus Christ: Grace to you and peace.

[2]We give thanks to God always for all of you, making mention of you in our prayers;

[3]constantly bearing in mind your work of faith and labor of love and steadfastness of hope in our Lord Jesus Christ in the presence of our God and Father,

[4]knowing, brethren beloved by God, His choice of you;

[5]for our gospel did not come to you in word only, but also in power and in the Holy Spirit and with full conviction; just as you know what kind of men we proved to be among you for your sake.

[6]You also became imitators of us and of the Lord, having received the word in much tribulation with the joy of the Holy Spirit,

[7]so that you became an example to all the believers in Macedonia and in Achaia.

[8]For the word of the Lord has sounded forth from you, not only in Macedonia and Achaia, but also in every place your faith toward God has gone forth, so that we have no need to say anything.

[9]For they themselves report about us what kind of a reception we had with you, and how you turned to Godfrom idols to serve a living and true God,

[10]and to wait for His Son from heaven, whom He raised from the dead, that is Jesus, who rescues us fromthe wrath to come.

1 Thessalonians 2

Paul's Ministry

[1]For you yourselves know, brethren, that our coming to you was not in vain,

[2]but after we had already suffered and been mistreated in Philippi, as you know, we had the boldness in our God to speak to you the gospel of God amid much opposition.

[3]For our exhortation does not come from error or impurity or by way of deceit;

⁴but just as we have been approved by God to be entrusted with the gospel, so we speak, not as pleasing men, but God who examines our hearts.

⁵For we never came with flattering speech, as you know, nor with a pretext for greed--God is witness--

⁶nor did we seek glory from men, either from you or from others, even though as apostles of Christ we might have asserted our authority.

⁷But we proved to be gentle among you, as a nursing mother tenderly cares for her own children.

⁸Having so fond an affection for you, we were well-pleased to impart to you not only the gospel of God but also our own lives, because you had become very dear to us.

⁹For you recall, brethren, our labor and hardship, how working night and day so as not to be a burden to any of you, we proclaimed to you the gospel of God.

¹⁰You are witnesses, and so is God, how devoutly and uprightly and blamelessly we behaved toward you believers;

¹¹just as you know how we were exhorting and encouraging and imploring each one of you as a father would his own children,

¹²so that you would walk in a manner worthy of the God who calls you into His own kingdom and glory.

¹³For this reason we also constantly thank God that when you received the word of God which you heard from us, you accepted it not as the word of men, but for what it really is, the word of God, which also performs its work in you who believe.

¹⁴For you, brethren, became imitators of the churches of God in Christ Jesus that are in Judea, for you also endured the same sufferings at the hands of your own countrymen, even as they did from the Jews,

¹⁵who both killed the Lord Jesus and the prophets, and drove us out. They are not pleasing to God, but hostile to all men,

¹⁶hindering us from speaking to the Gentiles so that they may be saved; with the result that they always fill up the measure of their sins But wrath has come upon them to the utmost.

¹⁷But we, brethren, having been taken away from you for a short while-- in person, not in spirit--were all the more eager with great desire to see your face.

[18]For we wanted to come to you--I, Paul, more than once--and yet Satan hindered us.

[19]For who is our hope or joy or crown of exultation? Is it not even you, in the presence of our Lord Jesus at His coming?

[20]For you are our glory and joy.

1 Thessalonians 3

Encouragement of Timothy's Visit

[1]Therefore when we could endure it no longer, we thought it best to be left behind at Athens alone,

[2]and we sent Timothy, our brother and God's fellow worker in the gospel of Christ, to strengthen and encourage you as to your faith,

[3]so that no one would be disturbed by these afflictions; for you yourselves know that we have been destined for this.

[4]For indeed when we were with you, we kept telling you in advance that we were going to suffer affliction; and so it came to pass, as you know.

[5]For this reason, when I could endure it no longer, I also sent to find out about your faith, for fear that the tempter might have tempted you, and our labor would be in vain.

[6]But now that Timothy has come to us from you, and has brought us good news of your faith and love, and that you alwaysthink kindly of us, longing to see us just as we also long to see you,

[7]for this reason, brethren, in all our distress and affliction we were comforted about you through your faith;

[8]for now we really live, if you stand firm in the Lord.

[9]For what thanks can we render to God for you in return for all the joy with which we rejoice before our God on your account,

[10]as we night and day keep praying most earnestly that we may see your face, and may complete what is lacking in your faith?

[11]Now may our God and Father Himself and Jesus our Lord direct our way to you;

[12]and may the Lord cause you to increase and abound in love for one another, and for all people, just as we also do for you;

[13]so that He may establish your hearts without blame in holiness be-

fore our God and Father at the coming of our Lord Jesuswith all His saints.

1 Thessalonians 4

Sanctification and Love

¹Finally then, brethren, we request and exhort you in the Lord Jesus, that as you received from us instruction as to how you ought to walk and please God (just as you actually do walk), that you excel still more.

²For you know what commandments we gave you by the authority of the Lord Jesus.

³For this is the will of God, your sanctification; that is, that you abstain from sexual immorality;

⁴that each of you know how to possess his own vessel in sanctification and honor,

⁵not in lustful passion, like the Gentiles who do not know God;

⁶and that no man transgress and defraud his brother in the matter because the Lord is the avenger in all these things, just as we also told you before and solemnly warned you.

⁷For God has not called us for the purpose of impurity, but in sanctification.

⁸So, he who rejects this is not rejecting man but the God who gives His Holy Spirit to you.

⁹Now as to the love of the brethren, you have no need for anyone to write to you, for you yourselves are taught by God to love one another;

¹⁰for indeed you do practice it toward all the brethren who are in all Macedonia But we urge you, brethren, to excel still more,

¹¹and to make it your ambition to lead a quiet life and attend to your own business and work with your hands, just as we commanded you,

¹²so that you will behave properly toward outsiders and not be in any need.

Those Who Died in Christ

¹³But we do not want you to be uninformed, brethren, about those who are asleep, so that you will not grieve as do the rest who have no hope.

¹⁴For if we believe that Jesus died and rose again, even so God will bring with Him those who have fallen asleep in Jesus.

¹⁵For this we say to you by the word of the Lord, that we who are alive and remain until the coming of the Lord, will not precede those who have fallen asleep.

¹⁶For the Lord Himself will descend from heaven with a shout, with the voice of the archangel and with the trumpet of God, and the dead in Christ will rise first.

¹⁷Then we who are alive and remain will be caught up together with them in the clouds to meet the Lord in the air, and so we shall always be with the Lord.

¹⁸Therefore comfort one another with these words.

1 Thessalonians 5

The Day of the Lord

¹Now as to the times and the epochs, brethren, you have no need of anything to be written to you.

²For you yourselves know full well that the day of the Lord will come just like a thief in the night.

³While they are saying, "Peace and safety!" then destruction will come upon them suddenly like labor pains upon a woman with child, and they will not escape.

⁴But you, brethren, are not in darkness, that the day would overtake you like a thief;

⁵for you are all sons of light and sons of day We are not of night nor of darkness;

⁶so then let us not sleep as others do, but let us be alert and sober.

⁷For those who sleep do their sleeping at night, and those who get drunk get drunk at night.

⁸But since we are of the day, let us be sober, having put on the breastplate of faith and love, and as a helmet, the hope of salvation.

⁹For God has not destined us for wrath, but for obtaining salvation through our Lord Jesus Christ,

¹⁰who died for us, so that whether we are awake or asleep, we will live together with Him.

[11]Therefore encourage one another and build up one another, just as you also are doing.

Christian Conduct

[12]But we request of you, brethren, that you appreciate those who diligently labor among you, and have charge over you in the Lord and give you instruction,

[13]and that you esteem them very highly in love because of their work. Live in peace with one another.

[14]We urge you, brethren, admonish the unruly, encourage the fainthearted, help the weak, be patient with everyone.

[15]See that no one repays another with evil for evil, but always seek after that which is good for one another and for all people.

[16]Rejoice always;

[17]pray without ceasing;

[18]in everything give thanks; for this is God's will for you in Christ Jesus.

[19]Do not quench the Spirit;

[20]do not despise prophetic utterances.

[21]But examine everything carefully; hold fast to that which is good;

[22]abstain from every form of evil.

[23]Now may the God of peace Himself sanctify you entirely; and may your spirit and soul and body be preserved complete,without blame at the coming of our Lord Jesus Christ.

[24]Faithful is He who calls you, and He also will bring it to pass.

[25]Brethren, pray for us.

[26]Greet all the brethren with a holy kiss.

[27]I adjure you by the Lord to have this letter read to all the brethren.

[28]The grace of our Lord Jesus Christ be with you.

OBSERVATION - WHAT DOES THE BIBLE SAY?
Structure - Part 1

Any writing, including the Bible, has basic principles of structure. Read through the description of each principle. We will be using examples from the record of the creation in Genesis 1:1-2:3.

(A copy of text in Genesis is at the end of this lesson. You can use it if you would like to practice marking the text.)

I. Repetition

Repetition is probably the most commonly used law of composition in the Bible. It is the mode of expression in which certain parts imitate or repeat one another. It is using the same or similar terms, phrases or ideas over and over. Repetition usually indicates importance.

A. What about the action of God is repeated in Genesis 1:3, 6, 9, 11, 14-15, 20, 24, 26, 29-30? _____

_____

_____

B. What did God see in Genesis 1:4, 10, 12, 18, 21, 25? _____

_____

_____

II. Progression

Progression is when the same theme runs throughout a passage. This theme is developed and built upon throughout the text. This progression usually leads to a climax.

Objective:

We would like to look at some of the basic ways that the words of the Bible are held together—principles of structure.

A.   What numbers lead us through the creation record?_____

_____

_____

B.   What progression is seen in the order of the things created?____

_____

_____

III.   Climax

Climax is an extension of progression. It is the building of thought to a peak of intensity. This peak is climax.

A.   As God inspected the creation (Genesis 1:4, 10, 12, 18, 21, 25) His inspection of the creation led to the climax of what pronouncement in verse 31?_____

_____

B.   Each thing created prepared the way for the next, leading to the climax of the creation of what in verse 26?_____

_____

C.   There also seems to be a climax in what happened on the seventh day. What is that climax?_____

_____

IV.   Contrast

Contrast is the association of opposites. The opposites help to define and emphasize each other.

A.   There is a contrast in what God did on days 1-6 and what was done on day 7. What was it? _____

_____

B.   What contrast is made concerning time in Genesis 1:5? "So the evening and the _____ ..."

C.   In Genesis 1:26, what is said about man that is not said about any other thing created?_____

_____

V.   Radiation

With radiation the author directs the eye to one point by making various truths converge upon, or issue from, that point. This principle is not used often and is much more involved.

A. In what way does everything radiate from God?_____

_____

B. Another example would be "the law of God" in Psalms 119.

C. Another example would be the throne of God in Revelation 4-5.

VI. Interchange

Interchange is where the author tells two stories side by side. This principle is not used frequently in Scripture.

A. There are no examples in the record of creation.

B. An example is found in Genesis 4:16-5:32. First, Cain's generations are recorded. Then, Adam's generations through Seth are recorded.

C. Glance over Luke 1:5-2:21. The births of two people are told side by side. Whose births are they?_____

_____

D. In 1 and 2 Kings, the histories of what two countries are recorded?_____

_____

The Creation of the World   *THE ENGLISH STANDARD VERSION*

1 In the beginning, God created the heavens and the earth. 2 The earth
was without form and void, and darkness was over the face of the deep. And the
Spirit of God was hovering over the face of the waters.

3 And God said, "Let there be light," and there was light. 4 And God saw that
the light was good. And God separated the light from the darkness. 5 God called
the light Day, and the darkness he called Night. And there was evening and there
was morning, the first day.

6 And God said, "Let there be an expanse1 in the midst of the waters, and let it
separate the waters from the waters." 7 And God made2 the expanse
and separated the waters that were under the expanse from the waters that
were above the expanse. And it was so.8 And God called the expanse
Heaven.3 And there was evening and there was morning, the second day.

9 And God said, "Let the waters under the heavens be gathered together into
one place, and let the dry land appear." And it was so.10 God called the dry land
Earth,4 and the waters that were gathered together he called Seas. And God saw
that it was good.

11 And God said, "Let the earth sprout vegetation, plants5 yielding seed, and
fruit trees bearing fruit in which is their seed, each according to its kind, on the
earth." And it was so. 12 The earth brought forth vegetation, plants yielding seed
according to their own kinds, and trees bearing fruit in which is their seed, each
according to its kind. And God saw that it was good. 13 And there was evening and
there was morning, the third day.

14 And God said, "Let there be lights in the expanse of the heavens to separate
the day from the night. And let them be for signs and for seasons,6 and for days
and years, 15 and let them be lights in the expanse of the heavens to give light
upon the earth." And it was so.16 And God made the two great lights—the greater
light to rule the day and the lesser light to rule the night—and the stars. 17 And
God set them in the expanse of the heavens to give light on the earth, 18 to rule
over the day and over the night, and to separate the light from the darkness. And
God saw that it was good. 19 And there was evening and there was morning, the
fourth day.

20 And God said, "Let the waters swarm with swarms of living creatures, and
let birds7 fly above the earth across the expanse of the heavens." 21 So God created the great sea creatures and every living creature that moves, with which the
waters swarm, according to their kinds, and every winged bird according to its
kind. And God saw that it was good. 22 And God blessed them, saying, "Be fruitful
and multiply and fill the waters in the seas, and let birds multiply on the
earth."23 And there was evening and there was morning, the fifth day.

24 And God said, "Let the earth bring forth living creatures according to their
kinds—livestock and creeping things and beasts of the earth according to their
kinds." And it was so. 25 And God made the beasts of the earth according to their
kinds and the livestock according to their kinds, and everything that creeps on the
ground according to its kind. And God saw that it was good.

26 Then God said, "Let us make man8 in our image, after our likeness. And let
them have dominion over the fish of the sea and over the birds of the heavens and

over the livestock and over all the earth and over every creeping thing that creeps on the earth."

27 So God created man in his own image, in the image of God he created him; male and female he created them.

28 And God blessed them. And God said to them, "Be fruitful and multiply and fill the earth and subdue it and have dominion over the fish of the sea and over the birds of the heavens and over every living thing that moves on the earth." 29 And God said, "Behold, I have given you every plant yielding seed that is on the face of all the earth, and every tree with seed in its fruit. You shall have them for food. 30 And to every beast of the earth and to every bird of the heavens and to everything that creeps on the earth, everything that has the breath of life, I have given every green plant for food." And it was so. 31 And God saw everything that he had made, and behold, it was very good. And there was evening and there was morning, the sixth day.

Footnotes
[1] **1:6** Or *a canopy*; also verses 7, 8, 14, 15, 17, 20
[2] **1:7** Or *fashioned*; also verse 16
[3] **1:8** Or *Sky*; also verses 9, 14, 15, 17, 20, 26, 28, 30; 2:1
[4] **1:10** Or *Land*; also verses 11, 12, 22, 24, 25, 26, 28, 30; 2:1
[5] **1:11** Or *small plants*; also verses 12, 29
[6] **1:14** Or *appointed times*
[7] **1:20** Or *flying things*; see Leviticus 11:19-20
[8] **1:26** The Hebrew word for *man* (*adam*) is the generic term for mankind and becomes the   proper name *Adam*

The Seventh Day, God Rests

2 Thus the heavens and the earth were finished, and all the host of them. 2 Thus the heavens and the earth were finished, and all the host of them. 2 And on the seventh day God finished his work that he had done, and he rested on the seventh day from all his work that he had done. 3 So God blessed the seventh day and made it holy, because on it God rested from all his work that he had done in creation.

The Creation of Man and Woman

4 These are the generations of the heavens and the earth when they were created, in the day that the LORD God made the earth and the heavens.

5 When no bush of the field1 was yet in the land2 and no small plant of the field had yet sprung up—for the LORD God had not caused it to rain on the land, and there was no man to work the ground, 6 and a mist3 was going up from the land and was watering the whole face of the ground— 7 then the LORD God formed the

man of dust from the ground and breathed into his nostrils the breath of life, and the man became a living creature. 8 And the LORD God planted a garden in Eden, in the east, and there he put the man whom he had formed. 9 And out of the ground the LORD God made to spring up every tree that is pleasant to the sight and good for food. The tree of life was in the midst of the garden, and the tree of the knowledge of good and evil.

10 A river flowed out of Eden to water the garden, and there it divided and became four rivers. 11 The name of the first is the Pishon. It is the one that flowed around the whole land of iHavilah, where there is gold. 12 And the gold of that land is good; bdellium and onyx stone are there. 13 The name of the second river is the Gihon. It is the one that flowed around the whole land of Cush. 14 And the name of the third river is the iTigris, which flows east of Assyria. And the fourth river is the Euphrates.

15 The LORD God took the man and put him in the garden of Eden to work it and keep it. 16 And the LORD God commanded the man, saying, "You may surely eat of every tree of the garden, 17 but of the tree of the knowledge of good and evil you shall not eat, for in the day that you eat4 of it you shall surely die."

18 Then the LORD God said, "It is not good that the man should be alone; I will make him a helper fit for5 him." 19 Now out of the ground the LORD God had formed6 every beast of the field and every bird of the heavens and brought them to the man to see what he would call them. And whatever the man called every living creature, that was its name. 20 The man gave names to all livestock and to the birds of the heavens and to every beast of the field. But for Adam7 there was not found a helper fit for him. 21 So the LORD God caused a deep sleep to fall upon the man, and while he slept took one of his ribs and closed up its place with flesh. 22 And the rib that the LORD God had taken from the man he made8 into a woman and brought her to the man. 23 Then the man said, "This at last is bone of my bones and flesh of my flesh; she shall be called Woman, because she was taken out of Man."9 24 Therefore a man shall leave his father and his mother and hold fast to his wife, and they shall become one flesh. 25 And the man and his wife were both naked and were not ashamed.

Footnotes

[1] **2:5** Or *open country*
[2] **2:5** Or *earth*; also verse 6
[3] **2:6** Or *spring*
[4] **2:17** Or *when you eat*
[5] **2:18** Or *corresponding to*; also verse 20
[6] **2:19** Or *And out of the ground the LORD God formed*
[7] **2:20** Or *the man*
[8] **2:22** Hebrew *built*
[9] **2:23** The Hebrew words for *woman* (*ishshah*) and *man* (*ish*) sound alike

OBSERVATION - WHAT DOES THE BIBLE SAY?
Structure - Part 2

Read through 1 Thessalonians and find examples of each of the principles of structure.

I.   Repetition

Repetition is probably the most commonly used law of composition in the Bible. It is the mode of expression in which certain parts imitate or repeat one another. It is using the same or similar terms, phrases or ideas over and over. Repetition usually indicates importance.

A. _____

_____

_____

B. _____

_____

_____

C. _____

_____

_____

D. _____

_____

_____

E. _____

_____

_____

Objective:

We would like to look at some of the basic ways that the words of the Bible are held together—principles of structure.

II.   Progression

Progression is when the same theme runs throughout a passage. This theme is developed and built upon throughout the text. This progression usually leads to a climax.

A. _____

_____

B. _____

_____

C. _____

_____

D. _____

_____

E. _____

_____

III.   Climax

Climax is an extension of progression. It is the building of thought to a peak of intensity. This peak is climax.

A. _____

_____

B. _____

_____

C. _____

_____

D. _____

_____

E. _____

_____

IV.   Contrast

Contrast is the association of opposites. The opposites help to define and emphasize each other.

A. _____

_____

B. _____

_____

C. _____

_____

D. _____

_____

E. _____

_____

V.   Radiation

With radiation the author directs the eye to one point by making various truths converge upon, or issue from, that point. You will not find any examples of this in 1 Thessalonians.

VI.   Interchange

Interchange is where the author tells two stories side by side. You will not find any examples of this in 1 Thessalonians.

OBSERVATION - WHAT DOES THE BIBLE SAY?
The Book of Ruth

Review lessons 2 through 7 and follow those principles in studying the book of Ruth. After reading and re-reading the book, record your observations on the next page of this lesson.

A copy of the text is found at the end of this lesson.

- Please note, you are reading another type of literature.

- Read a good introduction to this book.

- By the key verse of the book, write the word "key" or put a "key" symbol.

- Write above each chapter or division your summary statement.

- Use a pencil to underline the main story line.

- Put an asterisk, dot, or star by the main key words and phrases.

- At the beginning of the book, make a key to your system for this book.

- Mark your Bible with a color scheme that will help you see and remember the main thoughts of the book. (See the color scheme for Old Testament historical books in Lesson 5.)

What differences do you see between a letter like 1 Thessalonians and a historical narrative like Ruth?

_____

_____

_____

_____

_____

Objective:

In this lesson we would like to use what we have learned so far in studying a different type of book. Instead of looking at a letter like 1 Thessalonians, we will examine an Old Testament historical narrative—the book of Ruth.

Ruth 1

Naomi Widowed

[1]Now it came about in the days when the judges governed, that there was a fam-ine in the land And a certain man of Bethlehem in Judah went to sojourn in the land of Moab with his wife and his two sons.

[2]The name of the man was Elimelech, and the name of his wife, Naomi; and the names of his two sons were Mahlon and Chilion, Ephrathites of Bethlehem in Judah. Now theyentered the land of Moab and remained there.

[3]Then Elimelech, Naomi's husband, died; and she was left with her two sons.

[4]They took for themselves Moabite women as wives; the name of the one was Orpah and the name of the other Ruth. And they lived there about ten years.

[5]Then both Mahlon and Chilion also died, and the woman was bereft of her two children and her husband.

[6]Then she arose with her daughters-in-law that she might return from the land of Moab, for she had heard in the land of Moab that the LORD had visited His people in giving them food.

[7]So she departed from the place where she was, and her two daughters-in-law with her; and they went on the way to return to the land of Judah.

[8]And Naomi said to her two daughters-in-law, "Go, return each of you to her mother's house. May the LORD deal kindly with you as you have dealt with the dead and with me.

[9]"May the LORD grant that you may find rest, each in the house of her husband." Then she kissed them, and they lifted up their voices and wept.

[10]And they said to her, "No, but we will surely return with you to your people."

[11]But Naomi said, "Return, my daughters. Why should you go with me? Have I yet sons in my womb, that they may be your husbands?

[12]"Return, my daughters! Go, for I am too old to have a husband. If I said I have hope, if I should even have a husband tonight and also bear sons,

[13]would you therefore wait until they were grown? Would you therefore refrain from marrying? No, my daughters; for it is harder for me than for you, for the hand of the LORD has gone forth against me."

Ruth's Loyalty

[14]And they lifted up their voices and wept again; and Orpah kissed her mother-in-law, but Ruth clung to her.

[15]Then she said, "Behold, your sister-in-law has gone back to her people and her gods; return after your sister-in-law."

[16]But Ruth said, "Do not urge me to leave you or turn back from following you; for where you go, I will go, and where you lodge, I will lodge. Your people shall be my people, and your God, my God.

[17]"Where you die, I will die, and there I will be buried. Thus may the LORD do to me, and worse, if anything but death parts you and me."

[18]When she saw that she was determined to go with her, she said no more to her.

[19]So they both went until they came to Bethlehem. And when they had come to Bethlehem, all the city was stirred because of them, and the women said, "Is this Naomi?"

[20]She said to them, "Do not call me Naomi; call me Mara, for the Almighty has dealt very bitterly with me.

[21]"I went out full, but the LORD has brought me back empty. Why do you call me Naomi, since the LORD has witnessed against me and the Almighty has afflicted me?"

[22]So Naomi returned, and with her Ruth the Moabitess, her daughter-in-law, who returned from the land of Moab. And they came to Bethlehem at the beginning of barley harvest.

Ruth 2

Ruth Gleans in Boaz' Field

[1]Now Naomi had a kinsman of her husband, a man of great wealth, of the family of Elimelech, whose name was Boaz.

[2]And Ruth the Moabitess said to Naomi, "Please let me go to the field and glean among the ears of grain after one in whose sight I may find favor." And she said to her, "Go, my daughter."

[3]So she departed and went and gleaned in the field after the reapers; and she happened to come to the portion of the field belonging to Boaz, who was of the family of Elimelech.

[4]Now behold, Boaz came from Bethlehem and said to the reapers, "May the LORD be with you." And they said to him, "May the LORD bless you."

⁵Then Boaz said to his servant who was in charge of the reapers, "Whose young woman is this?"

⁶The servant in charge of the reapers replied, "She is the young Moabite woman who returned with Naomi from the land of Moab.

⁷"And she said, 'Please let me glean and gather after the reapers among the sheaves.' Thus she came and has remained from the morning until now; she has been sitting in the house for a little while."

⁸Then Boaz said to Ruth, "Listen carefully, my daughter. Do not go to glean in another field; furthermore, do not go on from this one, but stay here with my maids.

⁹"Let your eyes be on the field which they reap, and go after them. Indeed, I have commanded the servants not to touch you. When you are thirsty, go to the water jars and drink from what the servants draw."

¹⁰Then she fell on her face, bowing to the ground and said to him, "Why have I found favor in your sight that you should take notice of me, since I am a foreigner?"

¹¹Boaz replied to her, "All that you have done for your mother-in-law after the death of your husband has been fully reported to me, and how you left your father and your mother and the land of your birth, and came to a people that you did not previously know.

¹²"May the LORD reward your work, and your wages be full from the LORD, the God of Israel, under whose wings you have come to seek refuge."

¹³Then she said, "I have found favor in your sight, my lord, for you have comforted me and indeed have spoken kindly to your maidservant, though I am not like one of your maidservants."

¹⁴At mealtime Boaz said to her, "Come here, that you may eat of the bread and dip your piece of bread in the vinegar." So she sat beside the reapers; and he served her roasted grain, and she ate and was satisfied and had some left.

¹⁵When she rose to glean, Boaz commanded his servants, saying, "Let her glean even among the sheaves, and do not insult her.

¹⁶"Also you shall purposely pull out for her some grain from the bundles and leave it that she may glean, and do not rebuke her."

¹⁷So she gleaned in the field until evening. Then she beat out what she had gleaned, and it was about an ephah of barley.

¹⁸She took it up and went into the city, and her mother-in-law saw what she had

gleaned. She also took it out and gave Naomi what she had left after she was satisfied.

[19]Her mother-in-law then said to her, "Where did you glean today and where did you work? May he who took notice of you be blessed." So she told her mother-in-law with whom she had worked and said, "The name of the man with whom I worked today is Boaz."

[20]Naomi said to her daughter-in-law, "May he be blessed of the LORD who has not withdrawn his kindness to the living and to the dead." Again Naomi said to her, "The man is our relative, he is one of our closest relatives."

[21]Then Ruth the Moabitess said, "Furthermore, he said to me, 'You should stay close to my servants until they have finished all my harvest.'"

[22]Naomi said to Ruth her daughter-in-law, "It is good, my daughter, that you go out with his maids, so that others do not fall upon you in another field."

[23]So she stayed close by the maids of Boaz in order to glean until the end of the barley harvest and the wheat harvest. And she lived with her mother-in-law.

Ruth 3

Boaz Will Redeem Ruth

[1]Then Naomi her mother-in-law said to her, "My daughter, shall I not seek security for you, that it may be well with you?

[2]"Now is not Boaz our kinsman, with whose maids you were? Behold, he winnows barley at the threshing floor tonight.

[3]"Wash yourself therefore, and anoint yourself and put on your best clothes, and go down to the threshing floor; but do not make yourself known to the man until he has finished eating and drinking.

[4]"It shall be when he lies down, that you shall notice the place where he lies, and you shall go and uncover his feet and lie down; then he will tell you what you shall do."

[5]She said to her, "All that you say I will do."

[6]So she went down to the threshing floor and did according to all that her mother-in-law had commanded her.

[7]When Boaz had eaten and drunk and his heart was merry, he went to lie down at the end of the heap of grain; and she came secretly, and uncovered his feet and lay down.

[8]It happened in the middle of the night that the man was startled and bent forward; and behold, a woman was lying at his feet.

[9]He said, "Who are you?" And she answered, "I am Ruth your maid. So spread your covering over your maid, for you are a close relative."

[10]Then he said, "May you be blessed of the LORD, my daughter. You have shown your last kindness to be better than the first by not going after young men, whether poor or rich.

[11]"Now, my daughter, do not fear. I will do for you whatever you ask, for all my people in the city know that you are a woman of excellence.

[12]"Now it is true I am a close relative; however, there is a relative closer than I.

[13]"Remain this night, and when morning comes, if he will redeem you, good; let him redeem you But if he does not wish to redeem you, then I will redeem you, as the LORD lives. Lie down until morning."

[14]So she lay at his feet until morning and rose before one could recognize another; and he said, "Let it not be known that the woman came to the threshing floor."

[15]Again he said, "Give me the cloak that is on you and hold it." So she held it, and he measured six measures of barley and laid it on her. Then she went into the city.

[16]When she came to her mother-in-law, she said, "How did it go, my daughter?" And she told her all that the man had done for her.

[17]She said, "These six measures of barley he gave to me, for he said, 'Do not go to your mother-in-law empty-handed.'"

[18]Then she said, "Wait, my daughter, until you know how the matter turns out; for the man will not rest until he has settled it today."

Ruth 4

The Marriage of Ruth

[1]Now Boaz went up to the gate and sat down there, and behold, the close relative of whom Boaz spoke was passing by, so he said, "Turn aside, friend, sit down here." And he turned aside and sat down.

[2]He took ten men of the elders of the city and said, "Sit down here." So they sat down.

[3]Then he said to the closest relative, "Naomi, who has come back from the land of Moab, has to sell the piece of land which belonged to our brother Elimelech.

[4]"So I thought to inform you, saying, 'Buy it before those who are sitting here, and before the elders of my people If you will redeem it, redeem it; but if not, tell me that I may know; for there is no one but you to redeem it, and I am after you.'" And he said, "I will redeem it."

[5]Then Boaz said, "On the day you buy the field from the hand of Naomi, you must also acquire Ruth the Moabitess, the widow of the deceased, in order to raise up the name of the deceased on his inheritance."

[6]The closest relative said, "I cannot redeem it for myself, because I would jeopardize my own inheritance. Redeem it for yourself; you may have my right of redemption, for I cannot redeem it."

[7]Now this was the custom in former times in Israel concerning the redemption and the exchange of land to confirm any matter: a man removed his sandal and gave it to another; and this was the manner of attestation in Israel.

[8]So the closest relative said to Boaz, "Buy it for yourself." And he removed his sandal.

[9]Then Boaz said to the elders and all the people, "You are witnesses today that I have bought from the hand of Naomi all that belonged to Elimelech and all that belonged to Chilion and Mahlon.

[10]"Moreover, I have acquired Ruth the Moabitess, the widow of Mahlon, to be my wife in order to raise up the name of the deceased on his inheritance, so that the name of the deceased will not be cut off from his brothers or from the court of his birth place; you are witnesses today."

[11]All the people who were in the court, and the elders, said, "We are witnesses. May the LORD make the woman who is coming into your home like Rachel and Leah, both of whom built the house of Israel; and may you achieve wealth in Ephrathah and become famous in Bethlehem.

[12]"Moreover, may your house be like the house of Perez whom Tamar bore to Judah, through the offspring which the LORD will give you by this young woman."

[13]So Boaz took Ruth, and she became his wife, and he went in to her. And the LORD enabled her to conceive, and she gave birth to a son.

[14]Then the women said to Naomi, "Blessed is the LORD who has not left you without a redeemer today, and may his name become famous in Israel.

[15]"May he also be to you a restorer of life and a sustainer of your old age; for your daughter-in-law, who loves you and is better to you than seven sons, has given birth to him."

The Line of David Began Here

¹⁶Then Naomi took the child and laid him in her lap, and became his nurse.

¹⁷The neighbor women gave him a name, saying, "A son has been born to Naomi!" So they named him Obed. He is the father of Jesse, the father of David.

¹⁸Now these are the generations of Perez: to Perez was born Hezron,

¹⁹and to Hezron was born Ram, and to Ram, Amminadab,

²⁰and to Amminadab was born Nahshon, and to Nahshon, Salmon,

²¹and to Salmon was born Boaz, and to Boaz, Obed,

²²and to Obed was born Jesse, and to Jesse, David.

OBSERVATION - WHAT DOES THE BIBLE SAY?
The Book of Habakkuk

Review lessons 2 through 7 and follow those principles in studying the book of Habakkuk. After reading and re-reading the book, record your observations on the next page of this lesson.

A copy of the text is found at the end of this lesson.

- Please note, you are reading another type of literature.

- Read a good introduction to this book.

- By the key verse of the book, write the word "key" or put a "key" symbol.

- Write above each chapter or division your summary statement.

- Underline any phrases or sentences that will help you recall the theme of the paragraphs.

- Put an asterisk, dot, or star by the main key words and phrases.

- At the beginning of the book, make a key to your system for this book.

- Mark your Bible with a color scheme that will help you see and remember the main thoughts of the book. (See the color scheme for Old Testament prophetic books in Lesson 5.)

What differences do you see between a letter like 1 Thessalonians, a prophetic book like Habakkuk and a historical narrative like Ruth? _____
_____
_____
_____

Objective:

In this lesson we would like to use what we have learned so far in studying a different type of book. Instead of looking at a New Testament Letter like 1 Thessalonians, we will examine an Old Testament prophetic book—the book of Habakkuk.

1 Chaldeans Used to Punish Judah

1 The oracle which Habakkuk the prophet saw. 2 How long, O LORD, will I call for help, And You will not hear ? I cry out to You, "Violence !" Yet You do not save. 3 Why do You make me see iniquity, And cause me to look on wickedness ? Yes, destruction and violence are before me; Strife exists and contention arises. 4 Therefore the law is ignored And justice is never upheld. For the wicked surround the righteous; Therefore justice comes out perverted. 5 "Look among the nations ! Observe ! Be astonished ! Wonder ! Because I am doing something in your days - You would not believe if you were told. 6 "For behold, I am raising up the Chaldeans, That fierce and impetuous people Who march throughout the earth To seize dwelling places which are not theirs. 7 "They are dreaded and feared ; Their justice and authority originate with themselves. 8 "Their horses are swifter than leopards And keener than wolves in the evening. Their horsemen come galloping, Their horsemen come from afar ; They fly like an eagle swooping down to devour. 9 "All of them come for violence. Their horde of faces moves forward. They collect captives like sand. 10 "They mock at kings And rulers are a laughing matter to them. They laugh at every fortress And heap up rubble to capture it. 11 "Then they will sweep through like the wind and pass on. But they will be held guilty, They whose strength is their god." 12 Are You not from everlasting, O LORD, my God, my Holy One ? We will not die. You, O LORD, have appointed them to judge ; And You, O Rock, have established them to correct. 13 Your eyes are too pure to approve evil, And You can not look on wickedness with favor. Why do You look with favor On those who deal treacherously ? Why are You silent when the wicked swallow up Those more righteous than they? 14 Why have You made men like the fish of the sea, Like creeping things without a ruler over them? 15 The Chaldeans bring all of them up with a hook, Drag them away with their net, And gather them together in their fishing net. Therefore they rejoice and are glad. 16 Therefore they offer a sacrifice to their net And burn incense to their fishing net ; Because through these things their catch is large, And their food is plentiful. 17 Will they therefore empty their net And continually slay nations without sparing ?

2 God Answers the Prophet

1 I will stand on my guard post And station myself on the rampart ; And I will keep watch to see what He will speak to me, And how I may reply when I am reproved. **2** Then the LORD answered me and said, "Record the vision And inscribe it on tablets, That the one who reads it may run. **3** "For the vision is yet for the appointed time ; It hastens toward the goal and it will not fail. Though it tarries, wait for it; For it will certainly come, it will not delay. **4** "Behold, as for the proud one, His soul is not right within him; But the righteous will live by his faith. **5** "Furthermore, wine betrays the haughty man, So that he does not stay at home. He enlarges his appetite like Sheol, And he is like death, never satisfied. He also gathers to himself all nations And collects to himself all peoples. **6** "Will not all of these take up a taunt-song against him, Even mockery and insinuations against him And say, 'Woe to him who increases what is not his- For how long - And makes himself rich with loans ?' **7** "Will not your creditors rise up suddenly, And those who collect from you awaken ? Indeed, you will become plunder for them. **8** "Because you have looted many nations, All the remainder of the peoples will loot you- Because of human bloodshed and violence done to the land, To the town and all its inhabitants. **9** "Woe to him who gets evil gain for his house To put hisnest on high, To be delivered from the hand of calamity ! **10** "You have devised a shameful thing for your house By cutting off many peoples ; So you are sinning against yourself. **11** "Surely the stone will cry out from the wall, And the rafter will answer it from the framework. **12** "Woe to him who builds a city with bloodshed And founds a town with violence ! **13** "Is it not indeed from the LORD of hosts That peoples toil for fire, And nations grow weary for nothing ? **14** "For the earth will be filled With the knowledge of the glory of the LORD, As the waters cover the sea. **15** "Woe to you who make your neighbors drink, Who mix in your venom even to make them drunk So as to look on their nakedness ! **16** "You will be filled with disgrace rather than honor. Now you yourself drink and expose your own nakedness. The cup in the LORD'S right hand will come around to you, And utter disgrace will come upon your glory. **17** "For the violence done to Lebanon will over whelm you, And the devastation of its beasts by which you terrified them, Because of human bloodshed and violence done to the land, To

the town and all its inhabitants. **18** "What profit is the
idol when its maker has carved it, Or an image, a teacher of falsehood ? For
its maker trusts in his own handiwork When
he fashions speechless idols. **19** "Woe to him who says to a piece of wood,
'Awake !' To a mute stone, 'Arise !' And that is your teacher ? Behold, it
is overlaid with gold and silver, And there is no breath at all inside it. **20** "But
the LORD is in His holy temple. Let all the earth be silent before Him."

3 God's Deliverance of His People

1 A prayer of Habakkuk the prophet, according to Shigionoth. **2** LORD, I
have heard the report about You and I fear. O LORD, revive Your work in
the midst of the years, In the midst of the years make it known ;
In wrath remember mercy. **3** God comes from Teman, And the Holy One from
Mount Paran. Selah. His splendor covers the heavens, And the earth is full of
His praise. **4** His radiance is like the sunlight ; He has rays flashing from His hand,
And there is the hiding of His power. **5** Before Him goes pestilence,
And plague comes after Him. **6** He stood and surveyed the earth ;
He looked and startled the nations. Yes, the perpetual mountains were shattered,
The ancient hills collapsed.
His ways are everlasting. **7** I saw the tents of Cushan under distress, The
tent curtains of the land of Midian were trembling. **8** Did the LORD rage against
the rivers, Or was Your anger against the rivers, Or was Your wrath against the sea,
That You rode on Your horses, On
Your chariots of salvation ? **9** Your bow was made bare ,
The rods of chastisement were sworn. Selah.
You cleaved the earth with rivers. **10** The mountains saw You and quaked ; The
downpour of waters swept by. The deep uttered forth its voice,
It lifted high its hands. **11** Sun and moon stood in their places ; They went away at
the light of Your arrows, At the radiance of Your gleam-
ing spear. **12** In indignation You marched through the earth ;
In anger You trampled the nations. **13** You went forth for the salvation of
Your people, For the salvation of Your anointed. You struck the head of
the house of the evil To lay him open from thigh to neck. Selah. **14** You
pierced with his own spears The head of his throngs. They stormed in to scatter us;
Their exultation was like those
Who devour the oppressed in secret. **15** You trampled on the sea with Your horses,
On the surge of many waters. **16** I heard and my inward parts trembled, At

the sound my lips quivered. Decay enters my bones, And in
my place I tremble. Because I must wait quietly for the day of distress, For
the people to arise who will invade us. **17** Though the fig tree should
not blossom And there be no fruit on the vines, Though the yield of
the olive should fail And the fields produce no food, Though the flock should
be cut off from the fold And there be no cattle in the stalls, **18** Yet I will exult in
the LORD, I will rejoice in the God of my salvation. **19** The Lord GOD is my strength,
And He has made my feet like hinds' feet, And makes me walk on my high places.
For the choir director, on my stringed instruments.

OBSERVATION - WHAT DOES THE BIBLE SAY?
The Song of Solomon

Review lessons 2 through 7 and follow those principles in studying the book of Song of Solomon. After reading and re-reading the book, record your observations on the next page of this lesson.

A copy of the text is found at the end of this lesson.

- Please note, you are reading another type of literature.

- Read a good introduction to this book.

- By the key verse of the book, write the word "key" or put a "key" symbol.

- Write above each chapter or division your summary statement.

- Underline any phrases or sentences that will help you recall the theme of the paragraphs.

- Put an asterisk, dot, or star by the main key words and phrases.

- At the beginning of the book, make a key to your system for this book.

- Mark your Bible with a color scheme that will help you see and remember the main thoughts of the book. (See the color scheme for Old Testament poetic books in Lesson 5.)

What differences do you see between a letter like 1 Thessalonians, a historical narrative like Ruth, a prophetic book like Habakkuk and a poetic book like Song of Solomon?_____

_____

_____

_____

Objective:

In this lesson we would like to use what we have learned so far in studying a different type of book. We will examine an Old Testament book of poetry—the book of Song of Solomon.

Song of Solomon 1

The Young Shulammite Bride and Jerusalem's Daughters

¹The Song of Songs, which is Solomon's.
　　²"May he kiss me with the kisses of his mouth!
　　　　For your love is better than wine.
　　³"Your oils have a pleasing fragrance,
　　　　Your name is like purified oil;
　　　　Therefore the maidens love you.
　　⁴"Draw me after you and let us run together!
　　　　The king has brought me into his chambers "
　　　　"We will rejoice in you and be glad;
　　　　We will extol your love more than wine.
　　　　Rightly do they love you."
　　⁵"I am black but lovely,
　　　　O daughters of Jerusalem,
　　　　Like the tents of Kedar,
　　　　Like the curtains of Solomon.
　　⁶"Do not stare at me because I am swarthy,
　　　　For the sun has burned me.
　　　　My mother's sons were angry with me;
　　　　They made me caretaker of the vineyards,
　　　　But I have not taken care of my own vineyard.
　　⁷"Tell me, O you whom my soul loves,
　　　　Where do you pasture your flock,
　　　　Where do you make it lie down at noon?
　　　　For why should I be like one who veils herself
　　　　Beside the flocks of your companions?"

Solomon, the Lover, Speaks

　　⁸"If you yourself do not know,
　　　　Most beautiful among women,
　　　　Go forth on the trail of the flock
　　　　And pasture your young goats
　　　　By the tents of the shepherds.
　　⁹"To me, my darling, you are like
　　　　My mare among the chariots of Pharaoh.
　　¹⁰"Your cheeks are lovely with ornaments,
　　　　Your neck with strings of beads."
　　¹¹"We will make for you ornaments of gold
　　　　With beads of silver."
　　¹²"While the king was at his table,
　　　　My perfume gave forth its fragrance.
　　¹³"My beloved is to me a pouch of myrrh
　　　　Which lies all night between my breasts.
　　¹⁴"My beloved is to me a cluster of henna blossoms
　　　　In the vineyards of Engedi."
　　¹⁵"How beautiful you are, my darling,

> How beautiful you are!
>   Your eyes are like doves."
> [16]"How handsome you are, my beloved,
>   And so pleasant!
>   Indeed, our couch is luxuriant!
> [17]"The beams of our houses are cedars,
>   Our rafters, cypresses.
>
> ### Song of Solomon 2
>
> **The Bride's Admiration**
>
> [1]"I am the rose of Sharon,
>   The lily of the valleys."
> [2]"Like a lily among the thorns,
>   So is my darling among the maidens."
> [3]"Like an apple tree among the trees of the forest,
>   So is my beloved among the young men
>   In his shade I took great delight and sat down,
>   And his fruit was sweet to my taste.
> [4]"He has brought me to his banquet hall,
>   And his banner over me is love.
> [5]"Sustain me with raisin cakes,
>   Refresh me with apples,
>   Because I am lovesick.
> [6]"Let his left hand be under my head
>   And his right hand embrace me."
> [7]"I adjure you, O daughters of Jerusalem,
>   By the gazelles or by the hinds of the field,
>   That you do not arouse or awaken my love
>   Until she pleases."
> [8]"Listen! My beloved!
>   Behold, he is coming,
>   Climbing on the mountains,
>   Leaping on the hills!
> [9]"My beloved is like a gazelle or a young stag
>   Behold, he is standing behind our wall,
>   He is looking through the windows,
>   He is peering through the lattice.
> [10]"My beloved responded and said to me,
>   'Arise, my darling, my beautiful one,
>   And come along.
> [11]'For behold, the winter is past,
>   The rain is over and gone.
> [12]'The flowers have already appeared in the land;
>   The time has arrived for pruning the vines,
>   And the voice of the turtledove has been heard in our land.
> [13]'The fig tree has ripened its figs,
>   And the vines in blossom have given forth their fragrance.
>   Arise, my darling, my beautiful one,
>   And come along!'"
> [14]"O my dove, in the clefts of the rock,

In the secret place of the steep pathway,
Let me see your form,
Let me hear your voice;
For your voice is sweet,
And your form is lovely."
¹⁵"Catch the foxes for us,
The little foxes that are ruining the vineyards,
While our vineyards are in blossom."
¹⁶"My beloved is mine, and I am his;
He pastures his flock among the lilies.
¹⁷"Until the cool of the day when the shadows flee away,
Turn, my beloved, and be like a gazelle
Or a young stag on the mountains of Bether."

Song of Solomon 3

The Bride's Troubled Dream

¹"On my bed night after night I sought him
Whom my soul loves;
I sought him but did not find him.
²'I must arise now and go about the city;
In the streets and in the squares
I must seek him whom my soul loves.'
I sought him but did not find him.
³"The watchmen who make the rounds in the city found me,
And I said, 'Have you seen him whom my soul loves?'
⁴"Scarcely had I left them
When I found him whom my soul loves;
I held on to him and would not let him go
Until I had brought him to my mother's house,
And into the room of her who conceived me."
⁵"I adjure you, O daughters of Jerusalem,
By the gazelles or by the hinds of the field,
That you will not arouse or awaken my love
Until she pleases."

Solomon's Wedding Day

⁶"What is this coming up from the wilderness
Like columns of smoke,
Perfumed with myrrh and frankincense,
With all scented powders of the merchant?
⁷"Behold, it is the traveling couch of Solomon;
Sixty mighty men around it,
Of the mighty men of Israel.
⁸"All of them are wielders of the sword,
Expert in war;
Each man has his sword at his side,
Guarding against the terrors of the night.
⁹"King Solomon has made for himself a sedan chair
From the timber of Lebanon.

10"He made its posts of silver,
    Its back of gold
    And its seat of purple fabric,
    With its interior lovingly fitted out
    By the daughters of Jerusalem.
11"Go forth, O daughters of Zion,
    And gaze on King Solomon with the crown
    With which his mother has crowned him
    On the day of his wedding,
    And on the day of his gladness of heart."

Song of Solomon 4

Solomon's Love Expressed

1"How beautiful you are, my darling,
    How beautiful you are!
    Your eyes are like doves behind your veil;
    Your hair is like a flock of goats
    That have descended from Mount Gilead.
2"Your teeth are like a flock of newly shorn ewes
    Which have come up from their washing,
    All of which bear twins,
    And not one among them has lost her young.
3"Your lips are like a scarlet thread,
    And your mouth is lovely
    Your temples are like a slice of a pomegranate
    Behind your veil.
4"Your neck is like the tower of David,
    Built with rows of stones
    On which are hung a thousand shields,
    All the round shields of the mighty men.
5"Your two breasts are like two fawns,
    Twins of a gazelle
    Which feed among the lilies.
6"Until the cool of the day
    When the shadows flee away,
    I will go my way to the mountain of myrrh
    And to the hill of frankincense.
7"You are altogether beautiful, my darling,
    And there is no blemish in you.
8"Come with me from Lebanon, my bride,
    May you come with me from Lebanon
    Journey down from the summit of Amana,
    From the summit of Senir and Hermon,
    From the dens of lions,
    From the mountains of leopards.
9"You have made my heart beat faster, my sister, my bride;
    You have made my heart beat faster with a single glance of your eye
    With a single strand of your necklace.
10"How beautiful is your love, my sister, my bride!
    How much better is your love than wine,

And the fragrance of your oils
Than all kinds of spices!
11"Your lips, my bride, drip honey;
Honey and milk are under your tongue,
And the fragrance of your garments is like the fragrance of Lebanon.
12"A garden locked is my sister, my bride,
A rock garden locked, a spring sealed up.
13"Your shoots are an orchard of pomegranates
With choice fruits, henna with nard plants,
14Nard and saffron, calamus and cinnamon,
With all the trees of frankincense,
Myrrh and aloes, along with all the finest spices.
15"You are a garden spring,
A well of fresh water,
And streams flowing from Lebanon."
16"Awake, O north wind,
And come, wind of the south;
Make my garden breathe out fragrance,
Let its spices be wafted abroad
May my beloved come into his garden
And eat its choice fruits!"

Song of Solomon 5

The Torment of Separation

1"I have come into my garden, my sister, my bride;
I have gathered my myrrh along with my balsam
I have eaten my honeycomb and my honey;
I have drunk my wine and my milk
Eat, friends;
Drink and imbibe deeply, O lovers."
2"I was asleep but my heart was awake.
A voice! My beloved was knocking:
'Open to me, my sister, my darling,
My dove, my perfect one!
For my head is drenched with dew,
My locks with the damp of the night.'
3"I have taken off my dress,
How can I put it on again?
I have washed my feet,
How can I dirty them again?
4"My beloved extended his hand through the opening,
And my feelings were aroused for him.
5"I arose to open to my beloved;
And my hands dripped with myrrh,
And my fingers with liquid myrrh,
On the handles of the bolt.
6"I opened to my beloved,
But my beloved had turned away and had gone!
My heart went out to him as he spoke
I searched for him but I did not find him;

I called him but he did not answer me.
7"The watchmen who make the rounds in the city found me,
They struck me and wounded me;
The guardsmen of the walls took away my shawl from me.
8"I adjure you, O daughters of Jerusalem,
If you find my beloved,
As to what you will tell him:
For I am lovesick."
9"What kind of beloved is your beloved,
O most beautiful among women?
What kind of beloved is your beloved,
That thus you adjure us?"

Admiration by the Bride

10"My beloved is dazzling and ruddy,
Outstanding among ten thousand.
11"His head is like gold, pure gold;
His locks are like clusters of dates
And black as a raven.
12"His eyes are like doves
Beside streams of water,
Bathed in milk,
And reposed in their setting.
13"His cheeks are like a bed of balsam,
Banks of sweet-scented herbs;
His lips are lilies
Dripping with liquid myrrh.
14"His hands are rods of gold
Set with beryl;
His abdomen is carved ivory
Inlaid with sapphires.
15"His legs are pillars of alabaster
Set on pedestals of pure gold;
His appearance is like Lebanon
Choice as the cedars.
16"His mouth is full of sweetness
And he is wholly desirable.
This is my beloved and this is my friend,
O daughters of Jerusalem."

Song of Solomon 6

Mutual Delight in Each Other

1"Where has your beloved gone,
O most beautiful among women?
Where has your beloved turned,
That we may seek him with you?"
2"My beloved has gone down to his garden,
To the beds of balsam,
To pasture his flock in the gardens

And gather lilies.
[3]"I am my beloved's and my beloved is mine,
  He who pastures his flock among the lilies."
[4]"You are as beautiful as Tirzah, my darling,
  As lovely as Jerusalem,
  As awesome as an army with banners.
[5]"Turn your eyes away from me,
  For they have confused me;
  Your hair is like a flock of goats
  That have descended from Gilead.
[6]"Your teeth are like a flock of ewes
  Which have come up from their washing,
  All of which bear twins,
  And not one among them has lost her young.
[7]"Your temples are like a slice of a pomegranate
  Behind your veil.
[8]"There are sixty queens and eighty concubines,
  And maidens without number;
[9]But my dove, my perfect one, is unique:
  She is her mother's only daughter;
  She is the pure child of the one who bore her
  The maidens saw her and called her blessed,
  The queens and the concubines also, and they praised her, saying,
[10]'Who is this that grows like the dawn,
  As beautiful as the full moon,
  As pure as the sun,
  As awesome as an army with banners?'
[11]"I went down to the orchard of nut trees
  To see the blossoms of the valley,
  To see whether the vine had budded
  Or the pomegranates had bloomed.
[12]"Before I was aware, my soul set me
  Over the chariots of my noble people."
[13]"Come back, come back, O Shulammite;
  Come back, come back, that we may gaze at you!"
  "Why should you gaze at the Shulammite,
  As at the dance of the two companies?

Song of Solomon 7

Admiration by the Bridegroom

[1]"How beautiful are your feet in sandals,
  O prince's daughter!
  The curves of your hips are like jewels,
  The work of the hands of an artist.
[2]"Your navel is like a round goblet
  Which never lacks mixed wine;
  Your belly is like a heap of wheat
  Fenced about with lilies.
[3]"Your two breasts are like two fawns,
  Twins of a gazelle.

⁴"Your neck is like a tower of ivory,
        Your eyes like the pools in Heshbon
        By the gate of Bath-rabbim;
        Your nose is like the tower of Lebanon,
        Which faces toward Damascus.
⁵"Your head crowns you like Carmel,
        And the flowing locks of your head are like purple threads;
        The king is captivated by your tresses.
⁶"How beautiful and how delightful you are,
        My love, with all your charms!
⁷"Your stature is like a palm tree,
        And your breasts are like its clusters.
⁸"I said, 'I will climb the palm tree,
        I will take hold of its fruit stalks.'
        Oh, may your breasts be like clusters of the vine,
        And the fragrance of your breath like apples,
⁹And your mouth like the best wine!"
        "It goes down smoothly for my beloved,
        Flowing gently through the lips of those who fall asleep.

The Union of Love

¹⁰"I am my beloved's,
        And his desire is for me.
¹¹"Come, my beloved, let us go out into the country,
        Let us spend the night in the villages.
¹²"Let us rise early and go to the vineyards;
        Let us see whether the vine has budded
        And its blossoms have opened,
        And whether the pomegranates have bloomed.
        There I will give you my love.
¹³"The mandrakes have given forth fragrance;
        And over our doors are all choice fruits,
        Both new and old,
        Which I have saved up for you, my beloved.

Song of Solomon 8

The Lovers Speak

¹"Oh that you were like a brother to me
        Who nursed at my mother's breasts.
        If I found you outdoors, I would kiss you;
        No one would despise me, either.
²"I would lead you and bring you
        Into the house of my mother, who used to instruct me;
        I would give you spiced wine to drink from the juice of my pomegrar
³"Let his left hand be under my head
        And his right hand embrace me."
⁴"I want you to swear, O daughters of Jerusalem,
        Do not arouse or awaken my love
        Until she pleases."

⁵"Who is this coming up from the wilderness
   Leaning on her beloved?"
    "Beneath the apple tree I awakened you;
   There your mother was in labor with you,
   There she was in labor and gave you birth.
⁶"Put me like a seal over your heart,
   Like a seal on your arm
   For love is as strong as death,
   Jealousy is as severe as Sheol;
   Its flashes are flashes of fire,
   The very flame of the LORD.
⁷"Many waters cannot quench love,
   Nor will rivers overflow it;
   If a man were to give all the riches of his house for love,
   It would be utterly despised."
⁸"We have a little sister,
   And she has no breasts;
   What shall we do for our sister
   On the day when she is spoken for?
⁹"If she is a wall,
   We will build on her a battlement of silver;
   But if she is a door,
   We will barricade her with planks of cedar."
¹⁰"I was a wall, and my breasts were like towers;
   Then I became in his eyes as one who finds peace.
¹¹"Solomon had a vineyard at Baal-hamon;
   He entrusted the vineyard to caretakers
   Each one was to bring a thousand shekels of silver for its fruit.
¹²"My very own vineyard is at my disposal;
   The thousand shekels are for you, Solomon,
   And two hundred are for those who take care of its fruit."
¹³"O you who sit in the gardens,
   My companions are listening for your voice--
   Let me hear it!"
¹⁴"Hurry, my beloved,
   And be like a gazelle or a young stag
   On the mountains of spices."

OBSERVATION - WHAT DOES THE BIBLE SAY?
Matthew 5-7

Review lessons 2 through 7 and follow those principles in studying a section from book of Matthew, chapters 5-7. After reading and re-reading the section, record your observations on the next page of this lesson.

A copy of the text is found at the end of this lesson.

- Please note, you are reading another type of literature.

- Read a good introduction to this book.

- By the key verse of the book, write the word "key" or put a "key" symbol.

- Write above each chapter or division your summary statement.

- Underline any phrases or sentences that will help you recall the theme of the paragraphs.

- Put an asterisk, dot, or star by the main key words and phrases.

- At the beginning of the book, make a key to your system for this book.

- Mark your Bible with a color scheme that will help you see and remember the main thoughts of the book. (See the color scheme for New Testament Gospel/Law in Lesson 5.)

What differences do you see between a letter like 1 Thessalonians, a historical narrative like Ruth, a prophetic book like Habakkuk, a poetic book like Song of Solomon and a section of Law like Matthew 5-7?

_____

_____

_____

_____

Objective:

In this lesson we would like to use what we have learned so far in studying a different type of book. We will examine a New Testament section of Law/Gospel—Matthew 5-7.

MATTHEW 5-7 THE NEW AMERICAN STANDARD BIBLE

Matthew 5

The Sermon on the Mount; The Beatitudes

[1]When Jesus saw the crowds, He went up on the mountain; and after He sat down, His disciples came to Him.

[2]He opened His mouth and began to teach them, saying,

[3]"Blessed are the poor in spirit, for theirs is the kingdom of heaven.

[4]"Blessed are those who mourn, for they shall be comforted.

[5]"Blessed are the gentle, for they shall inherit the earth.

[6]"Blessed are those who hunger and thirst for righteousness, for they shall be satisfied.

[7]"Blessed are the merciful, for they shall receive mercy.

[8]"Blessed are the pure in heart, for they shall see God.

[9]"Blessed are the peacemakers, for they shall be called sons of God.

[10]"Blessed are those who have been persecuted for the sake of righteousness, for theirs is the kingdom of heaven.

[11]"Blessed are you when people insult you and persecute you, and falsely say all kinds of evil against you because of Me.

[12]"Rejoice and be glad, for your reward in heaven is great; for in the same way they persecuted the prophets who were before you.

Disciples and the World

[13]"You are the salt of the earth; but if the salt has become tasteless, how can it be made salty again? It is no longer good for anything, except to be thrown out and trampled under foot by men.

[14]"You are the light of the world. A city set on a hill cannot be hidden;

[15]nor does anyone light a lamp and put it under a basket, but on the lampstand, and it gives light to all who are in the house.

[16]"Let your light shine before men in such a way that they may see your good

works, and glorify your Father who is in heaven.

[17]"Do not think that I came to abolish the Law or the Prophets; I did not come to abolish but to fulfill.

[18]"For truly I say to you, until heaven and earth pass away, not the smallest letter or stroke shall pass from the Law until all is accomplished.

[19]"Whoever then annuls one of the least of these commandments, and teaches others to do the same, shall be called least in the kingdom of heaven; but whoever keeps and teaches them, he shall be called great in the kingdom of heaven.

[20]"For I say to you that unless your righteousness surpasses that of the scribes and Pharisees, you will not enter the kingdom of heaven.

Personal Relationships

[21]"You have heard that the ancients were told, 'YOU SHALL NOT COMMIT MURDER' and 'Whoever commits murder shall beliable to the court.'

[22]"But I say to you that everyone who is angry with his brother shall be guilty before the court; and whoever says to his brother, 'You good-for-nothing,' shall be guilty before the supreme court; and whoever says, 'You fool,' shall be guilty enough to go into the fiery hell.

[23]"Therefore if you are presenting your offering at the altar, and there remember that your brother has something against you,

[24]leave your offering there before the altar and go; first be reconciled to your brother, and then come and present your offering.

[25]"Make friends quickly with your opponent at law while you are with him on the way, so that your opponent may not hand you over to the judge, and the judge to the officer, and you be thrown into prison.

[26]"Truly I say to you, you will not come out of there until you have paid up the last cent.

[27]"You have heard that it was said, 'YOU SHALL NOT COMMIT ADULTERY';

[28]but I say to you that everyone who looks at a woman with lust for her has already committed adultery with her in his heart.

[29]"If your right eye makes you stumble, tear it out and throw it from you; for it is better for you to lose one of the parts of your body, than for your whole body to be thrown into hell.

[30]"If your right hand makes you stumble, cut it off and throw it from you; for it is better for you to lose one of the parts of your body, than for your whole body to go into hell.

[31]"It was said, 'WHOEVER SENDS HIS WIFE AWAY, LET HIM GIVE HER A CERTIFI-CATE OF DIVORCE';

[32]but I say to you that everyone who divorces his wife, except for the reason of unchastity, makes her commit adultery; and whoever marries a divorced woman commits adultery.

[33]"Again, you have heard that the ancients were told, 'YOU SHALL NOT MAKE FALSE VOWS, BUT SHALL FULFILL YOUR VOWS TO THE LORD.'

[34]"But I say to you, make no oath at all, either by heaven, for it is the throne of God,

[35]or by the earth, for it is the footstool of His feet, or by Jerusalem, for it is THE CITY OF THE GREAT KING.

[36]"Nor shall you make an oath by your head, for you cannot make one hair white or black.

[37]"But let your statement be, 'Yes, yes' or 'No, no'; anything beyond these is of evil.

[38]"You have heard that it was said, 'AN EYE FOR AN EYE, AND A TOOTH FOR A TOOTH.'

[39]"But I say to you, do not resist an evil person; but whoever slaps you on your right cheek, turn the other to him also.

[40]"If anyone wants to sue you and take your shirt, let him have your coat also.

[41]"Whoever forces you to go one mile, go with him two.

[42]"Give to him who asks of you, and do not turn away from him who wants to bor-row from you.

[43]"You have heard that it was said, 'YOU SHALL LOVE YOUR NEIGHBOR and hate your enemy.'

[44]"But I say to you, love your enemies and pray for those who persecute you,

[45]so that you may be sons of your Father who is in heaven; for He causes His sun to rise on the evil and the good, and sends rain on the righteous and the unrighte-ous.

[46]"For if you love those who love you, what reward do you have? Do not even the tax collectors do the same?

[47]"If you greet only your brothers, what more are you doing than others? Do not even the Gentiles do the same?

[48]"Therefore you are to be perfect, as your heavenly Father is perfect.

Matthew 6

Giving to the Poor and Prayer

[1]"Beware of practicing your righteousness before men to be noticed by them; otherwise you have no reward with your Father who is in heaven.

[2]"So when you give to the poor, do not sound a trumpet before you, as the hypocrites do in the synagogues and in the streets, so that they may be honored by men Truly I say to you, they have their reward in full.

[3]"But when you give to the poor, do not let your left hand know what your right hand is doing,

[4]so that your giving will be in secret; and your Father who sees what is done in secret will reward you.

[5]"When you pray, you are not to be like the hypocrites; for they love to stand and pray in the synagogues and on the street corners so that they may be seen by men Truly I say to you, they have their reward in full.

[6]"But you, when you pray, go into your inner room, close your door and pray to your Father who is in secret, and your Father who sees what is done in secret will reward you.

[7]"And when you are praying, do not use meaningless repetition as the Gentiles do, for they suppose that they will be heard for their many words.

[8]"So do not be like them; for your Father knows what you need before you ask Him.

[9]"Pray, then, in this way:
    'Our Father who is in heaven,
    Hallowed be Your name.
  [10]'Your kingdom come
    Your will be done,
    On earth as it is in heaven.
  [11]'Give us this day our daily bread.
  [12]'And forgive us our debts, as we also have forgiven our debtors.

¹³'And do not lead us into temptation, but deliver us from evil. [For Yours is the kingdom and the power and the glory forever. Amen.]'

¹⁴"For if you forgive others for their transgressions, your heavenly Father will also forgive you.

¹⁵"But if you do not forgive others, then your Father will not forgive your transgressions.

Fasting; The True Treasure; Wealth (Mammon)

¹⁶"Whenever you fast, do not put on a gloomy face as the hypocrites do, for they neglect their appearance so that they will be noticed by men when they are fasting Truly I say to you, they have their reward in full.

¹⁷"But you, when you fast, anoint your head and wash your face

¹⁸so that your fasting will not be noticed by men, but by your Father who is in secret; and your Father who sees what is done in secret will reward you.

¹⁹"Do not store up for yourselves treasures on earth, where moth and rust destroy, and where thieves break in and steal.

²⁰"But store up for yourselves treasures in heaven, where neither moth nor rust destroys, and where thieves do not break in or steal;

²¹for where your treasure is, there your heart will be also.

²²"The eye is the lamp of the body; so then if your eye is clear, your whole body will be full of light.

²³"But if your eye is bad, your whole body will be full of darkness. If then the light that is in you is darkness, how great is the darkness!

²⁴"No one can serve two masters; for either he will hate the one and love the other, or he will be devoted to one and despise the other You cannot serve God and wealth.

The Cure for Anxiety

²⁵"For this reason I say to you, do not be worried about your life, as to what you will eat or what you will drink; nor for your body, as to what you will put on. Is not life more than food, and the body more than clothing?

²⁶"Look at the birds of the air, that they do not sow, nor reap nor gather into barns, and yet your heavenly Father feeds them. Are you not worth much more than they?

[27]"And who of you by being worried can add a single hour to his life?

[28]"And why are you worried about clothing? Observe how the lilies of the field grow; they do not toil nor do they spin,

[29]yet I say to you that not even Solomon in all his glory clothed himself like one of these.

[30]"But if God so clothes the grass of the field, which is alive today and tomorrow is thrown into the furnace, will He not much more clothe you? You of little faith!

[31]"Do not worry then, saying, 'What will we eat?' or 'What will we drink?' or 'What will we wear for clothing?'

[32]"For the Gentiles eagerly seek all these things; for your heavenly Father knows that you need all these things.

[33]"But seek first His kingdom and His righteousness, and all these things will be added to you.

[34]"So do not worry about tomorrow; for tomorrow will care for itself. Each day has enough trouble of its own.

Matthew 7

Judging Others

[1]"Do not judge so that you will not be judged.

[2]"For in the way you judge, you will be judged; and by your standard of measure, it will be measured to you.

[3]"Why do you look at the speck that is in your brother's eye, but do not notice the log that is in your own eye?

[4]"Or how can you say to your brother, 'Let me take the speck out of your eye,' and behold, the log is in your own eye?

[5]"You hypocrite, first take the log out of your own eye, and then you will see clearly to take the speck out of your brother's eye.

[6]"Do not give what is holy to dogs, and do not throw your pearls before swine, or they will trample them under their feet, and turn and tear you to pieces.

Prayer and the Golden Rule

[7]"Ask, and it will be given to you; seek, and you will find; knock, and it will be

opened to you.

[8]"For everyone who asks receives, and he who seeks finds, and to him who knocks it will be opened.

[9]"Or what man is there among you who, when his son asks for a loaf, will give him a stone?

[10]"Or if he asks for a fish, he will not give him a snake, will he?

[11]"If you then, being evil, know how to give good gifts to your children, how much more will your Father who is in heaven give what is good to those who ask Him!

[12]"In everything, therefore, treat people the same way you want them to treat you, for this is the Law and the Prophets.

The Narrow and Wide Gates

[13]"Enter through the narrow gate; for the gate is wide and the way is broad that leads to destruction, and there are many who enter through it.

[14]"For the gate is small and the way is narrow that leads to life, and there are few who find it.

A Tree and Its Fruit

[15]"Beware of the false prophets, who come to you in sheep's clothing, but inwardly are ravenous wolves.

[16]"You will know them by their fruits. Grapes are not gathered from thorn bushes nor figs from thistles, are they?

[17]"So every good tree bears good fruit, but the bad tree bears bad fruit.

[18]"A good tree cannot produce bad fruit, nor can a bad tree produce good fruit.

[19]"Every tree that does not bear good fruit is cut down and thrown into the fire.

[20]"So then, you will know them by their fruits.

[21]"Not everyone who says to Me, 'Lord, Lord,' will enter the kingdom of heaven, but he who does the will of My Father who is in heaven will enter.

[22]"Many will say to Me on that day, 'Lord, Lord, did we not prophesy in Your name, and in Your name cast out demons, and in Your name perform many miracles?'

[23]"And then I will declare to them, 'I never knew you; DEPART FROM ME, YOU

WHO PRACTICE LAWLESSNESS.'

The Two Foundations

[24]"Therefore everyone who hears these words of Mine and acts on them, may be compared to a wise man who built his house on the rock.

[25]"And the rain fell, and the floods came, and the winds blew and slammed against that house; and yet it did not fall, for it had been founded on the rock.

[26]"Everyone who hears these words of Mine and does not act on them, will be like a foolish man who built his house on the sand.

[27]"The rain fell, and the floods came, and the winds blew and slammed against that house; and it fell--and great was its fall."

[28]When Jesus had finished these words, the crowds were amazed at His teaching;

[29]for He was teaching them as one having authority, and not as their scribes.

INTERPRETATION - WHAT DOES IT MEAN?
Context, Context, Context - Part 1

It seems that an elderly mountain farmer in a muledrawn wagon had been involved in an accident with an automobile. Now, he was suing the driver, claiming personal injuries.

"But isn't it true that after the accident," the defendant's attorney asked, "you said you never felt better in your life?"

"Well," the claimant began, "that morning I got up, hitched up my mule, put my hound dog in the wagon, and jest got over the rise in the road when this big car barreled into my rear end.

"My mule was knocked to one side of the road, my hound dog to the other, and I was pinned under the seat. Directly a police came along, seen my mule had its leg broke, pulled out his pistol and shot it dead. He went over to my dog, seen it was hurt bad, and shot it in the head.

"Then," the farmer continued, "he come over to me and asked, "Well, how are you feelin'?' and, shore enough, I said, 'I never felt better in my life!'" (Robert Turner, from *Plain Talk* Vol. 9 No. 10 p. 8)

Objective:

In this lesson, we would like to stress the importance of context and how it affects our interpretation.

I.   **Context**

A.   Context is that which goes around the text.

1.   Everything in the Bible is in the context of the Bible as a whole, the book in which it is found and the immediate surrounding text.

        a.   Remember in particular the theme of the book, the section summary and the flow of thought as you try to understand any particular verse.

    2.   No interpretation of a passage should contradict or be out of harmony with any other plain passage in the Bible, the book or the immediate surrounding text.

        a.   No passage should be used to make a point that is not made by the text, even if it is otherwise true.

B.   Examples to illustrate the need to remember context.

    1.   What does the word "world" mean in John 3:16? _____
_____
_____

    2.   What does the word "world" mean in 1 John 2:15? _____
_____
_____

    3.   What does the phrase "fallen asleep" in 1 Thessalonians 4:13 mean? _____
_____
_____

II. How to determine context

(We will use 1 Thessalonians 1:9-10 to illustrate these principles. Please read and re-read 1 Thessalonians 1-3 in preparation for our discussion.)

A.   Keep the **flow and progression** of the passage in mind.

    1.   How does the point of this passage fit into the whole?

    2.   What main point is being made?

    3.   Where is the thought of the passage going?

B.   Keep the **original readers** in mind.

    1.   What did this passage mean to the people to whom it was written?

    2.   Try to see the passage through their culture and background before you see it through yours.

C.   Let the **author interpret** the passage for you as much as possible.

1. Why would the writer say this? In what tone do you hear him writing this?

2. How does this thought harmonize with what is being said overall?

D. Look for **special pointers**.

   1. Summary statements

      a. Words like "therefore," "so" or "if then" will sometimes signal a summary statement.

      b. With these summaries, the writer emphasizes what he wants emphasized.

   2. Explanations of why something is said

      a. Words like "for," "that" or "because" sometimes signal that the writer is explaining why he is saying something.

E. Keep in mind **other passages** in the Bible that have a similar or common theme.

   1. The Bible does not reveal every detail in every verse. Much of Bible study is the pulling in of many passages to get a complete picture of a particular subject.

   2. Many times we might not understand a particular passage fully. Understand it as much as possible and file it away in your memory. One day you will be reading another passage and you will say, "Now I see! That's how it fits together."

INTERPRETATION - WHAT DOES IT MEAN?

Context, Context, Context - Part 2

Please review the principles we examined in our last lesson and explain the meaning of the following passages. Be careful not to jump to the application of these passages. We will examine application in a later lesson.

1 Thessalonians 4:15

"...we who are alive and remain until the coming of the Lord, will by no means precede those who are asleep."

1. How does this fit into the flow and progression of the book?_____
    _____
    _____
    _____

2. What did this mean to the original readers?
    _____
    _____
    _____
    _____

3. How did Paul help to interpret this passage for us?_____
    _____
    _____
    _____
    _____

4. Are there any "special pointers"?_____
    _____
    _____
    _____
    _____

Objective:

In this lesson, we would like to interpret some portions of 1 Thessalonians.

5. What does it mean? _____

    _____

    _____

6. (Optional) What other passages in the Bible might help us understand
    this passage? _____

    _____

    _____

1 Thessalonians 4:3

"For this is the will of God, your sanctification..."

1. How does this fit into the flow and progression of the book? _____

    _____

    _____

2. What did this mean to the original readers? _____

    _____

    _____

3. How did Paul help to interpret this passage for us? _____

    _____

    _____

4. Are there any "special pointers"? _____

    _____

    _____

5. What does it mean? _____

    _____

    _____

6. (Optional) What other passages in the Bible might help us understand
    this passage? _____

    _____

    _____

INTERPRETATION - WHAT DOES IT MEAN?
Figures of Speech - Part 1

Please read the definitions given for each type of figure and find an example of it in the verse listed. (These definitions are taken from *How to Study Your Bible* by Kay Arthur.)

I.   **Simile**

"A simile is an expressed or stated comparison of two different things or ideas that uses the connecting words *like, as, such as* or the word pair *as...so*."

A.   Revelation 1:14 _____

_____

_____

(see also Psalms 42:1; Colossians 3:13)

II.   **Metaphor**

"A metaphor is an implied comparison between two things that are different. A metaphor is different from a simile in that a metaphor is not a *stated* comparison; it is an *implied* comparison. In a metaphor the words of comparison *like, as*, and *such as* are not used." The object being compared (literal) and the comparison (figure) are stated.

A.   John 15:5_____

_____

_____

_____

(see also Ephesians 6:17; Colossians 4:6)

Objective:

To look at figurative language used in the Bible and how to interpret it.

III.   Metonymy

"Metonymy is a figure of association, when the name of one object or concept is used for that of another to which it is related." The object being compared (literal) is not stated. Only the comparison (figure) is stated.

A.   Mark 1:5 _____

_____

_____

(see also Luke 22:20, 42; Acts 2:34-35)

IV.   Exaggeration

"Exaggeration, also called hyperbole, is a deliberate exaggeration for effect or emphasis. Hyperboles are found in all languages. However, they are frequently used among Semitic people, and that's what the children of Israel were—Semitic people."

A.   Matthew 23:24 _____

_____

_____

(see also Psalms 119:20; Judges 7:12; Jeremiah 9:1)

V.   Synecdoche

"Synecdoche is another figure of association where the whole can refer to the part or the part to the whole."

A.   Colossians 4:18 _____

_____

_____

(see also Acts 20:7; Colossians 1:20)

VI.   Personification

"In personification an object is given characteristics or attributes that belong to people."

A.   Proverbs 1:20 _____

_____

_____

(see also Isaiah 55:12)

VII. **Irony**

"Irony is a statement which says the opposite of what is meant. Irony is used for emphasis or effect."

A.   1 Corinthians 4:8 _____

_____

_____

VIII. **Parable**

"A parable is a story that teaches a moral lesson or truth. Although it is not usually factual, a parable is a story that is true to life. It is designed to make one central point, and every detail of the parable will reinforce that main point."

A.   Matthew 13 _____

_____

_____

IX. **Allegory**

"An allegory is a story with an underlying meaning that differs from the surface facts or the story itself; in other words, it describes one thing by using the image of another. Some refer to an allegory as an extended metaphor."

A.   Galatians 4:21-31 _____

_____

_____

X. **Type/Antitype, Shadow/Reality**

"A type is a prophetic symbol designated by God. A type prefigures something or someone to come. That which it prefigures is called an antitype." Be careful to let God identify which are types and which are not.

A.   Hebrews 10:1 _____

_____

_____

(see also Romans 5:14; Colossians 2:16-17)

INTERPRETATION - WHAT DOES IT MEAN?
Figures of Speech - Part 2

Please review the definitions given for each type of figure from lesson 11. Read the book of 1 Thessalonians and record what firgurative language you find. (There will not be examples of all of these types.)

I.   Simile
"A simile is an expressed or stated comparison of two different things or ideas that uses the connecting words *like, as, such as* or the word pair *as...so.*"

_____
_____
_____
_____
_____

Objective:

To look at figurative language used in the book of 1 Thessalonians.

II.   Metaphor
"A metaphor is an implied comparison between two things that are different. A metaphor is different from a simile in that a metaphor is not a *stated* comparison; it is an *implied* comparison. In a metaphor the words of comparison *like, as,* and *such as* are not used." The object being compared (literal) and the comparison (figure) are stated.

_____
_____
_____
_____
_____

III.   Metonymy

"Metonymy is a figure of association, when the name of one object or concept is used for that of another to which it is related." The object being compared (literal) is not stated. Only the comparison (figure) is stated._____

_____

_____

_____

IV.   Exaggeration

"Exaggeration, also called hyperbole, is a deliberate exaggeration for effect or emphasis. Hyperboles are found in all languages. However, they are frequently used among Semitic people, and that's what the children of Israel were—Semitic people."_____

_____

_____

_____

_____

V.   Synecdoche

"Synecdoche is another figure of association where the whole can refer to the part or the part to the whole."_____

_____

_____

_____

_____

VI.   Personification

"In personification an object is given characteristics or attributes that belong to people." _____

_____

_____

_____

_____

VII.   Irony

"Irony is a statement which says the opposite of what is meant. Irony is used for emphasis or effect."_____

_____

_____

_____

_____

VIII. Parable

"A parable is a story that teaches a moral lesson or truth. Although it is not usually factual, a parable is a story that is true to life. It is designed to make one central point, and every detail of the parable will reinforce that main point." _____

_____
_____
_____
_____

IX. Allegory

"An allegory is a story with an underlying meaning that differs from the surface facts or the story itself; in other words, it describes one thing by using the image of another. Some refer to an allegory as an extended metaphor." _____

_____
_____
_____
_____

X. Type/Antitype, Shadow/Reality

"A type is a prophetic symbol designated by God. A type prefigures something or someone to come. That which it prefigures is called an antitype." Be careful to let God identify which are types and which are not. _____

_____
_____
_____
_____

INTERPRETATION - WHAT DOES IT MEAN?
Basic Helps - Part 1

I.   **Cross-references**

A.   Cross-references help us find passages that are related to one another in some way. Sometimes the passage referenced contains the same idea, refers to the same event or is a quotation.

B.   Read through 1 Thessalonians 4:1-8, you will see verses referenced at the end of each verse, in a center or side column. The publishers of your Bible have placed these references there. There will be some symbol in the passage which shows which phrase is being referenced.

1.   If you are unsure of the system your Bible uses, see the page of explanation in the front of the Bible.

C.   This is one way to let scripture interpret scripture. As you read other passages that relate to the passage you are studying, the Bible helps interpret itself.

1.   This is particularly true when looking at OT passages. If it is explained in the NT, we have a Divine commentary on the passage.

a.   Example: Peter explains Psalm 16:8-11 in Acts 2:25-32.

2.   These references are also helpful in gathering all the Bible says on a particular subject.

Objective:

To introduce some of the basic tools of Bible study.

D. It is helpful to develop your own cross-reference system.

    1. In pencil, write in your margin passages that relate to the one you are studying.

        a. For example, write 1 Thessalonians 4:3 in 1 Corinthians 6:15's margin and visa versa.

        b. Write it down, because the related passage that seems so obvious to you now may be forgotten later.

II. Concordances

A. A concordance is an alphabetical listing of words, with their occurrences, in the Bible.

    1. It is especially helpful when you have a passage in mind but do not know where it is. Look up any word in the verse and scan through its occurrences until you find the passage you are looking for.

    2. It is also helpful when determining the meaning of a word as it is used in the Bible.

B. Find the word "sanctification" in the concordance in your Bible.

    1. Your concordance will contain some occurrences of often used words.

C. An "exhaustive" concordance shows all of the occurrences of all words.

    1. Remember that a concordance deals with a specific translation. If you are using a different translation, the words will not always be the same.

    2. How to use: (Illustrate with *Strong's Exhaustive Concordance*— see sample #1 on page 102.)

        a. Look up "sanctification" in the concordance.

            (1) You will find every time that word is found in the Bible.

            (2) You will see the scripture reference, phrase where the word occurs and a number.

        b. Find the number to the right of the scripture reference. This number corresponds to the Hebrew (OT) or Greek (NT) word that is found in the passage.

c. In the back of the concordance you will find the number in the Hebrew or Greek dictionary. (See sample #2 on page 103.)

d. Note: The numbers found in *Strong's* are used in several other reference works. It is, therefore, not necessary to be able to read the Hebrew or Greek word to find this number in other books.

III. Topical Indexes/Bibles

A. A topical index/Bible lists passages by topics or subjects.

1. It differs from a concordance in that passages are arranged by a topic or idea, rather than by a particular word.

2. It also differs in that the topic may include passages where the idea occurs even though the particular word does not

B. Find "sanctification" in the topical index in your Bible.

C. It is also possible to buy entire books which topically arrange passages. *Nave's Topical Bible* is very good (it uses KJV in its references). (See sample #3 on page 104.)

D. How to use:

1. Subjects are arranged in alphabetical order. Look up your subject.

2. You will find a listing of related passages.

3. If there are many passages, there may be some outline to the organization of the passages as well.

Strong's Exhaustive Concordance

34 Then *S·* went to Ramah; and Saul "
35 *S·* came no more to see Saul until "
35 nevertheless *S·* mourned for Saul: "
16: 1 the Lord said unto *S·*, How long "
2 And *S·* said, How can I go? if Saul "
4 *S·* did that which the Lord spake, "
7 Lord said unto *S·*, Look not on his "
8 and made him pass before *S·*. "
10 seven of his sons to pass before *S·*. "
10 *S·* said unto Jesse, The Lord hath "
11 *S·* said unto Jesse, Are here all thy "
11 *S·* said unto Jesse, Send and fetch "
13 Then *S·* took the horn of oil, and "
13 So *S·* rose up, and went to Ramah. "
19:18 escaped, and came to *S·* to Ramah, "
18 he and *S·* went and dwelt in Naioth."
20 *S·* standing as appointed over them," "
22 and said, Where are *S·* and David? "
24 and prophesied before *S·* in like "
25: 1 And *S·* died; and all the Israelites "
28: 3 Now *S·* was dead, and all Israel had"
11 thee? And he said, Bring me up *S·*. "
12 when the woman saw *S·*, she cried "
14 And Saul perceived that it was *S·*, "
15 *S·* said to Saul, Why hast thou"
16 Then said *S·*, Wherefore then dost "
20 afraid, because of the words of *S·*: "
1Ch 6:28 the sons of *S·*; the firstborn Vashni," "
9:22 David and *S·* the seer did ordain "
11: 3 to the word of the Lord by *S·*. "
26:28 And all that *S·* the seer, and Saul "
29:29 written in the book of *S·* the seer, "
2Ch 35:18 from the days of *S·* the prophet: "
Ps 99: 6 and *S·* among them that call upon "
Jer 15: 1 Though Moses and *S·* stood before "
Ac 3:24 Yea, and all the prophets from *S·* *4545*
13:20 and fifty years, until *S·* the prophet." "
Heb11: 32 of David also, and *S·*, and of the "

Sanballat   (*san-bal'-lat*)
Ne 2:10 When *S·* the Horonite, and Tobiah5571
19 when *S·* the Horonite, and Tobiah "
4: 1 when *S·* heard that we builded the "
7 to pass, that when *S·*, and Tobiah, "
6: 1 came to pass, when *S·*, and Tobiah," "
2 That *S·* and Geshem sent unto me "
5 Then sent *S·* his servant unto me "
12 for Tobiah and *S·* had hired him. "
14 God, think thou upon Tobiah and *S·*"
13: 28 was son in law to *S·* the Horonite: "

sanctification
1Co 1: 30 righteousness,...*s·*, and redemption: *38*
1Th 4: 3 this is the will of God, even your *s·*, "
4 possess his vessel in *s·* and honour: "
2Th 2:13 to salvation through *s·* of the Spirit "
1Pe 1: 2 Father, through *s·* of the Spirit, unto"

→ **sanctified**
Ge 2: 3 blessed the seventh day, and *s·* it:*6942

14 perfected for ever them that are *s·*. "
29 of the covenant, wherewith he was *s·*," "
Jude 1 them that are *s·* by God the Father,* "

sanctifieth
M't 23:17 gold, or the temple that *s·* the gold?*37
19 the gift, or the altar that *s·* the gift? "
Heb 2:11 and they who are sanctified "
9:13 *s·* to the purifying of the flesh: * "

sanctify   See also SANCTIFIED; SANCTIFIETH.
Ex 13: 2 *S·* unto me all the firstborn,   6942
19:10 and *s·* them to day and to morrow, "
22 let the priests...*s·* themselves, "
23 bounds about the mount, and *s·* it. "
28:41 and consecrate them, and *s·* them, "
29:27 *s·* the breast of the wave offering, "
33 made, to consecrate and to *s·* them:" "
36 it, and thou shalt anoint it, to *s·* it. "
37 atonement for the altar, and *s·* it; "
44 And I will *s·* the tabernacle of the "
44 I will *s·* also both Aaron and his sons," "
30:29 And thou shalt *s·* them, that they "
31:13 that I am the Lord that doth *s·* you. "
40:10 and all his vessels, and *s·* the altar:" "
11 shall anoint the laver...and *s·* it. "
13 and anoint him, and *s·* him: "
Le 8:11 the laver and his foot, to *s·* them. "
12 head, and anointed him, to *s·* him. "
11:44 ye shall therefore *s·* yourselves, "
20: 7 *S·* yourselves therefore, and be ye "
8 them: I am the Lord which *s·* you. "
21: 8 Thou shalt *s·* him therefore; for he "
8 I the Lord, which *s·* you, am holy. "
15 his people: for I the Lord do *s·* him." "
23 for I the Lord do *s·* them. "
22: 9 profane it: I the Lord do *s·* them. "
16 things; for I the Lord do *s·* them. "
27:14 when a man shall *s·* his house to "
16 a man shall *s·* unto the Lord some "
17 If he *s·* his field from the year of "
18 if he *s·* his field after the jubile, "
22 if a man *s·* unto the Lord a field "
26 Lord's firstling, no man shall *s·* it; "
Nu 11:18 *S·* yourselves against to morrow, "
20:12 *s·* me in the eyes of the children of "
27:14 *s·* me at the water before their eyes:" "
De 5:12 Keep the sabbath day to *s·* it, as the*"
15:19 shalt *s·* unto the Lord thy God: "
Jos 3: 5 said unto the people, *S·* yourselves:" "
7:13 Up, *s·* the people, and say, "
13 *S·* yourselves against to morrow: "
1Sa 16: 5 *s·* yourselves, and come with me to "
1Ch 15:12 *s·* yourselves, both ye and your "
23:13 he should *s·* the most holy things, "
2Ch 29: 5 me, ye Levites, *s·* now yourse'ves, "
5 and *s·* the house of the Lord God of" "
17 first day of the first month to *s·*, "
34 upright in heart to *s·* themselves "

Strong's Greek Dictionary of the New Testament

A.

N. B.—The numbers *not in italics* refer to the words in the *Hebrew Dictionary*. Significations within quotation-marks are derivative representatives of the Greek.

1. Α a, *al'-fah;* of Heb. or.; the first letter of the alphabet; fig. only (from its use as a numeral) the *first;*—Alpha. Often used (usually ἀν **an,** before a vowel) also in composition (as a contraction from *427*) in the sense of *privation;* so in many words beginning with this letter; occasionally in the sense of *union* (as a contraction of *260*).

2. Ἀαρών **Aarōn,** *ah-ar-ōhn';* of Heb. or. [175]; *Aaron,* the brother of Moses:—Aaron.

3. Ἀβαδδών **Abaddōn** *ab-ad-dōhn';* of Heb. or. [11]; a *destroying angel:*—Abaddon.

4. ἀβαρής **abarēs,** *ab-ar-ace';* from *1* (as a neg. particle) and *922; weightless,* i.e. (fig.) *not burdensome:*—from being burdensome.

5. Ἀββᾶ **Abba,** *ab-bah';* of Chald. or. [2]; *father* (as a voc.):—Abba.

6. Ἄβελ **Abĕl,** *ab'-el;* of Heb. or. [1893]; *Abel,* the son of Adam:—Abel.

7. Ἀβιά **Abia,** *ab-ee-ah';* of Heb. or. [29]; *Abijah,* the name of two Isr.:—Abia.

8. Ἀβιάθαρ **Abiathar,** *ab-ee-ath'-ar;* of Heb. or. [54]; *Abiathar,* an Isr.:—Abiathar.

9. Ἀβιληνή **Abilēnē,** *ab-ee-lay-nay';* of for. or. [comp. 58]; *Abilene,* a region of Syria:—Abilene.

10. Ἀβιούδ **Abioud',** *ab-ee-ood';* of Heb. or. [31]; *Abihud,* an Isr.:—Abiud.

11. Ἀβραάμ **Abraam,** *ab-rah-am';* of Heb. or. [85]; *Abraham,* the Heb. patriarch:—Abraham. [In Acts 7 : 16 the text should prob. read *Jacob.*]

12. ἄβυσσος **abussŏs,** *ab'-us-sos;* from *1* (as a neg. particle) and a var. of *1037; depthless,* i.e. (spec.) (infernal) "*abyss*":—deep, (bottomless) pit.

13. Ἄγαβος **Agabŏs,** *ag'-ab-os;* of Heb. or. [comp. 2285]; *Agabus,* an Isr.:—Agabus.

14. ἀγαθοεργέω **agathŏĕrgĕō,** *ag-ath-er-gheh'-o;* from *18* and *2041;* to *work good:*—do good.

15. ἀγαθοποιέω **agathŏpŏiĕō,** *ag-ath-op-oy-eh'-o;* from *17;* to *be a well-doer* (as a favor or a duty):—(when) do good (well).

16. ἀγαθοποιΐα **agathŏpŏiïa,** *ag-ath-op-oy-ee'-ah;* from *17; well-doing,* i.e. *virtue:*—well-doing.

17. ἀγαθοποιός **agathŏpŏiŏs,** *ag-ath-op-oy-os';* from *18* and *4160;* a *well-doer,* i.e. *virtuous:*—them that do well.

18. ἀγαθός **agathŏs,** *ag-ath-os';* a prim. word; "*good*" (in any sense, often as noun):—benefit, good (-s, things), well. Comp. *2570.*

24. ἀγανάκτησις **aganaktēsis,** *ag-an-ak'-tay-sis;* from *23; indignation:*—indignation.

25. ἀγαπάω **agapaō,** *ag-ap-ah'-o;* perh. from ἄγαν **agan** (*much*) [or comp. 5689]; to *love* (in a social or moral sense):—(be-) love (-ed). Comp. *5368.*

26. ἀγάπη **agapē,** *ag-ah'-pay;* from *25; love,* i.e. *affection* or *benevolence;* spec. (plur.) a *love-feast:*—(feast of) charity ([-ably]), dear, love.

27. ἀγαπητός **agapētŏs,** *ag-ap-ay-tos';* from *25; beloved:*—(dearly, well) beloved, dear.

28. Ἄγαρ **Agar,** *ag'-ar;* of Heb. or. [1904]; *Hagar,* the concubine of Abraham:—Hagar.

29. ἀγγαρεύω **aggarĕuō,** *ang-ar-yew'-o;* of for. or. [comp. 104]; prop. to *be a courier,* i.e., (by impl.) to *press* into public service:—compel (to go).

30. ἀγγεῖον **aggĕiŏn,** *ang-eye'-on;* from ἄγγος **aggŏs** (a *pail,* perh. as *bent;* comp. the base of *43);* a *receptacle:*—vessel.

31. ἀγγελία **aggĕlia,** *ang-el-ee'-ah;* from *32;* an *announcement,* i.e. (by impl.) *precept:*—message.

32. ἄγγελος **aggĕlŏs,** *ang'-el-os;* from ἀγγέλλω **aggĕllō** [prob. der. from *71;* comp. *34*] (to *bring tidings*); a *messenger;* esp. an "*angel*"; by impl. a *pastor:*—angel, messenger.

33. ἄγε **agĕ,** *ag'-eh;* imper. of *71;* prop. *lead,* i.e. *come on:*—go to.

34. ἀγέλη **agĕlē,** *ag-el'-ay;* from *71* [comp. *32*]; a *drove:*—herd.

35. ἀγενεαλόγητος **agĕnĕalŏgētŏs,** *ag-en-eh-al-og'-ay-tos;* from *1* (as neg. particle) and *1075; unregistered* as to birth:—without descent.

36. ἀγενής **agĕnēs,** *ag-en-ace';* from *1* (as neg. particle) and *1085;* prop. *without kin,* i.e. (of unknown descent, and by impl.) *ignoble:*—base things.

37. ἁγιάζω **hagiazō,** *hag-ee-ad'-zo;* from *40;* to *make holy,* i.e. (cer.) *purify* or *consecrate;* (mentally) to *venerate:*—hallow, be holy, sanctify.

38. ἁγιασμός **hagiasmŏs,** *hag-ee-as-mos';* from *37;* prop. *purification,* i.e. (the state) *purity;* concr. (by Hebr.) a *purifier:*—holiness, sanctification. ←

39. ἅγιον **hagiŏn,** *hag'-ee-on;* neut. of *40;* a *sacred* thing (i.e. *spot*):—holiest (of all), holy place, sanctuary.

40. ἅγιος **hagiŏs,** *hag'-ee-os;* from ἄγος **hagŏs** (an *awful* thing) [comp. *53, 2282*]; *sacred* (phys. *pure,* mor. *blameless* or *religious,* cer. *consecrated*):—(most) holy (one, thing), saint.

41. ἁγιότης **hagiŏtēs,** *hag-ee-ot'-ace;* from *40; sanctity* (i.e. prop. the state):—holiness.

Nave's Topical Bible

in Israel, 1 Sam. 8:1-3. People desire a king; he protests, 1 Sam. 8:4-22. Anoints Saul king of Israel, 1 Sam. 9; 10. Renews the kingdom of Saul, 1 Sam. 11:12-15. Reproves Saul; foretells that his kingdom shall not be established, 1 Sam. 13:11-15; 15. Anoints David to be king, 1 Sam. 16. Shelters David when escaping from Saul, 1 Sam. 19:18. Death of; the lament for him, 1 Sam. 25:1. Called up by the witch of Endor, 1 Sam. 28:3-20. His integrity as judge and ruler, 1 Sam. 12:1-5; Psa. 99:6; Jer. 15:1; Heb. 11:32. Chronicles of, 1 Chr. 29:29. Sons of, 1 Chr. 6:28,33. Called SHEMUEL, 1 Chr. 6:33.

SANBALLAT, an enemy of the Jews in rebuilding Jerusalem after the captivity, Neh. 2:10,19; 4; 6; 13:28.

→ **SANCTIFICATION.** Firstborn of Israelites sanctified, Ex. 13:2. All Israel sanctified, Ex. 19:10,14. Material things sanctified by anointing, Ex. 40:9-11. The Lord the sanctifier, Ex. 31:13; Lev. 20:8; 21:8; 22:9. The altar sanctifies the gift, Ex. 29:37; 30:29. Tabernacle sanctified by God's presence, Ex. 29:43; 40:34,35.

UNCLASSIFIED SCRIPTURES RELATING TO: Ex. 31:13. Verily my sabbaths ye shall keep: for it *is* a sign between me and you throughout your generations; that *ye* may know that I *am* the LORD that doth sanctify you.

Ex. 33:16. For wherein shall it be known here that I and thy people have found grace in thy sight? *is it* not in that thou goest with us? so shall we be separated, I and thy people, from all the people that *are* upon the face of the earth.

Lev. 21:1. And the LORD said unto Moses, Speak unto the priests the sons of Aaron, and say unto them, There shall none be defiled for the dead among his people: 2. But for his kin, that is near unto him, *that is,* for his mother, and for his father, and for his son, and for his daughter, and for his

with fire. 10. And *he that is* the high priest among his brethren, upon whose head the anointing oil was poured, and that is consecrated to put on the garments, shall not uncover his head, nor rend his clothes; 11. Neither shall he go in to any dead body, nor defile himself for his father, or for his mother; 12. Neither shall he go out of the sanctuary, nor profane the sanctuary of his God; for the crown of the anointing oil of his God *is* upon him: I *am* the LORD. 13. And he shall take a wife in her virginity. 14. A widow, or a divorced woman, or profane, *or* an harlot, these shall he not take: but he shall take a virgin of his own people to wife. 15. Neither shall he profane his seed among his people: for I the LORD do sanctify him. 16. And the LORD spake unto Moses, saying, 17. Speak unto Aaron, saying, Whosoever *he be* of thy seed in their generations that hath *any* blemish, let him not approach to offer the bread of his God. 18. For whatsoever man *he be* that hath a blemish, he shall not approach: a blind man, or a lame, or he that hath a flat nose, or any thing superfluous, 19. Or a man that is brokenfooted, or brokenhanded, 20. Or crookbackt, or a dwarf, or that hath a blemish in his eye, or be scurvy, or scabbed, or hath his stones broken; 21. No man that hath a blemish of the seed of Aaron the priest shall come nigh to offer the offerings of the LORD made by fire: he hath a blemish; he shall not come nigh to offer the bread of his God. 22. He shall eat the bread of his God, *both* of the most holy, and of the holy. 23. Only he shall not go in unto the vail, nor come nigh unto the altar, because he hath a blemish; that he profane not my sanctuaries: for I the LORD do sanctify them.

Jer. 1:5. Before I formed thee in the belly I knew thee; and before thou camest forth out of the womb I sanctified thee, *and* I ordained thee a prophet unto the nations.

Ezek. 37:28. And the heathen shall know

INTERPRETATION - WHAT DOES IT MEAN?
Basic Helps - Part 2

IV. Dictionaries/Encyclopedias

A. A lexicon is a Hebrew or Greek dictionary. (The definitions found here are usually much more extensive than the ones in the back of a concordance.)

1. These definitions are based on word usage at the time of writing.

   a. Because of this, a Greek lexicon of New Testament words will be different from a dictionary of modern Greek.

   b. In many, you will also find a listing of Greek writings of the first century where this word can be found.

2. *Thayer's Greek Lexicon* is a very good work and some of the editions use *Strong's* numbering system.

3. If you have one at home, please look through it. If not, see page 108.

4. There is usually a distinction made between the definition of the word and the author's comments. Keep this distinction in mind.

5. How to use:

   a. Look up the Greek word (or *Strong's* number). Read the definition.

Objective:

To introduce some of the basic tools of Bible study.

        b. As with any language, there may be several definitions for the same word. Find the definition that fits the context of your passage. (In *Thayer's Lexicon*, there is an "*" if every passage is mentioned in which the word is found.)

B. An expository dictionary is a dictionary in which words are defined according to biblical usage (see page 109).

    1. It differs from a lexicon in that you look up the English word rather than the Hebrew or Greek word. Under the English word is found the different Hebrew or Greek words from which the word is translated.

    2. *Vine's Expository Dictionary of O.T. and N.T. Words* is very good (it uses KJV as key). *Zodhiates' The Complete Word Study Dictionary: N.T.* is keyed to *Strong's* numbers. *Wilson's O.T. Word Study* is good for the O.T. (it uses KJV as key).

        a. A 3-volume set of much more extensive definitions for N.T. words is *The New International Dictionary of New Testament Theology* edited by Colin Brown.

        b. A 2-volume set for O.T. words is the *Theological Workbook of the Old Testament* edited by Harris, Archer, and Waltke.

    3. How to use:

        a. Look up the English word.

        b. Find the part of speech: noun, verb, etc. (In *Vine's* there is a "¶" if every passage is mentioned in which the word is found.)

        c. Find the corresponding Greek word. Some *Vine's* use *Strong's* numbering system.

        d. In the back of *Vine's* is a listing of all the ways each Greek word is translated (in KJV).

C. A Bible dictionary is where you find people, places and events which are found in the Bible.

    1. For example, you would find articles on Jerusalem, Solomon and Philippians but not definitions for anxiety, fear or contentment.

        a. The *Zondervan Pictorial Bible Dictionary* is a good one (see page 110).

D. A Bible encyclopedia is similar to the Bible dictionary only much more detail is given.

1. The *Zondervan Pictorial Encyclopedia of the Bible* is very good. An older but more conservative set is *The International Standard Bible Encyclopaedia*.

V. Commentaries

A. A commentary contains the comments of a man on a particular text. It is arranged by book, chapter and verse rather than by subject or specific words.

B. How to use: (If you have a commentary, please get it out and look through it. If not, see page 111.)

1. Look up the desired passage in the commentary. Usually the chapter and verse references will be on the top of the page.

a. Sometimes a commentator will also have an overview at the beginning or end of each chapter.

b. There is also a discussion of the book's author, date, information about its recipients, as well as the circumstances surrounding its writing found at the beginning of each book.

2. Read the commentators comments.

a. He may refer to the cultural context, significance of the meaning of a particular word, other related texts and/or his observations and interpretations of the text.

b. Keep in mind the biases and prejudices of each commentator.

V.I Software

A. There are several programs developed for the computer which can aid in Bible study.

1. E-Sword (free): www.e-sword.net

2. Logos Bible Software is more expensive but well-made.

B. There are also many websites that are helpful.

1. biblicalstudies.info—Ferrell Jenkins' website contains a great deal of helpful information as well as many helpful links.

2. www.biblegateway.com—Search several versions of the Bible and additional material.

3. www.collegepress.com—Run by the Christian Church. Free downloads including the Bible Study Textbook series of commentaries found under "Additional Resources."

Thayer's Lexicon

, (plur. ἄγγη), i. q. ἀγγεῖον q. v.: Mt.
I. (From Hom. down; [cf. *Rutherford*,
23].) *
impv. of ἄγω), *come.' come now.'* used,
he classics (W. 516 (481)), even when
addressed: Jas. iv. 13; v. 1.*
ἄγω to drive), *a herd*: Mt. viii. 30 sqq.;
k. viii. 32 sq. (From Hom. down.) *
-ον, ὁ, (γενεαλογέω), *of whose descent*
unt (in the O. T.), [R. V. *without gene-*
i. 3 (vs. 6 μὴ γενεαλογούμενος). No-
prof. auth.*
ῦς), ὁ, ἡ, (γένος), opp. to εὐγενής, *of no
base birth*, a man of no name or repu-
d by prof. writ., also in the secondary
wardly, mean, base. In the N. T. only
ἀγενῆ τοῦ κόσμου i. e. those who among
no account; on the use of a neut. adj.
s, see W. 178 (167); [B. 122 (107)].*
ἡγίασα; Pass., [pres. ἁγιάζομαι]; pf. ἡγί-
άσθην; a word for which the Greeks use
freq. in bibl. (as equiv. to קָדַשׁ, שׁ הִקְדִּישׁ)
to make ἅγιον, *render* or *declare sacred*
te. Hence it denotes   **1.** *to render
to be venerable, to hallow* : τὸ ὄνομα τοῦ
so of God, Is. xxix. 23; Ezek. xx. 41;
. xxxiii. (xxxvi.) 4); [Lk. xi. 2]; τὸν
i. 15 (R G θεόν).   Since the stamp
sses over from the holiness of God to
ny connection with God, ἁγιάζειν de-
*arate from things profane and dedicate to
e and so render inviolable;*   **a.** t h i n g s
τὰ ἀρσενικά, Deut. xv. 19; ἡμέραν, Ex.
hr. vii. 16, etc.): τὸν χρυσόν, Mt. xxiii.
19; σκεῦος, 2 Tim. ii. 21.   **b.** p e r s o n s.
id by undergoing death to consecrate
whose will he in that way fulfils, Jn.
said ἁγιάσαι Christ, i. e. to have selected
ice (cf. ἀφορίζειν, Gal. i. 15) by having
m the office of Messiah, Jn. x. 36, cf.
xvi. 12 [ἐξ αὐτῶν ἡγίασε, καὶ πρὸς αὐτὸν
lection of men for the priesthood]; xlv.

[q. v.]); Rev. xxii. 11.   In general, Christians are
called ἡγιασμένοι [cf. Deut. xxxiii. 3], as those who,
freed from the impurity of wickedness, have been
brought near to God by their faith and sanctity, Acts
xx. 32; xxvi. 18.   In 1 Co. vii. 14 ἁγιάζεσθαι is used in
a peculiar sense of those who, although not Christians
themselves, are yet, by marriage with a Christian, withdrawn from the contamination of heathen impiety and
brought under the saving influence of the Holy Spirit dis-
playing itself among Christians; cf. Neander ad loc.*

ἁγιασμός, -οῦ, ὁ, a word used only by bibl. and eccl.   **38**
writ. (for in Diod. 4, 39; Dion. Hal. 1, 21, ἁγισμός is
the more correct reading), signifying   **1.** *consecration,
purification*, τὸ ἁγιάζειν.   **2.** the effect of consecration :
sanctification of heart and life, 1 Co. i. 30 (Christ is he to
whom we are indebted for sanctification); 1 Th. iv. 7;
Ro. vi. 19, 22; 1 Tim. ii. 15; Heb. xii. 14; ἁγιασμὸς
πνεύματος sanctification wrought by the Holy Spirit, 2 Th.
ii. 13; 1 Pet. i. 2.   It is opposed to lust in 1 Th. iv. 3 sq.
(It is used in a ritual sense, Judg. xvii. 3 [Alex.]; Ezek.
xlv. 4; [Am. ii. 11]; Sir. vii. 31, etc.)   [On its use in
the N. T. cf. Ellic. on 1 Th. iv. 3; iii. 13.]*

ἅγιος, -α, -ον, (fr. τὸ ἄγος religious awe, reverence;   **39-40**
ἄζω, ἄζομαι, to venerate, revere, esp. the gods, parents,
[Curtius § 118]), rare in prof. auth.; very frequent in
the sacred writ.; in the Sept. for קָדְושׁ;   **1.** properly
reverend, worthy of veneration : τὸ ὄνομα τοῦ θεοῦ, Lk. i.
49; God, on account of his incomparable majesty, Rev.
iv. 8 (Is. vi. 3, etc.), i. q. ἔνδοξος.   Hence used   **a.** of
t h i n g s which on account of some connection with God
possess a certain distinction and claim to reverence, as
places sacred to God which are not to be profaned,
Acts vii. 33; τόπος ἅγιος the temple, Mt. xxiv. 15 (on
which pass. see βδέλυγμα, c.); Acts vi. 13; xxi. 28; the
holy land or Palestine, 2 Macc. i. 29; ii. 18; τὸ ἅγιον and
τὰ ἅγια [W. 177 (167)] the temple, Heb. ix. 1, 24 (cf.
Bleek on Heb. vol. ii. 2, p. 477 sq.) ; spec. that part of
the temple or tabernacle which is called 'the holy
place' (מִקְדָּשׁ, Ezek. xxxvii. 28; xlv. 18), Heb. ix. 2
[here Rec. reads ἁγία]; ἅγια ἁγίων [W. 246 (231), cf. Ex.
xxix. 37; xxx. 10, etc.] the most hallowed portion of
the temple, 'the holy of holies,' (Ex. xxvi. 33 [cf. Joseph.

Vine's Expository Dictionary

SANCTIFICATION, SANCTIFY

A. Noun.

HAGIASMOS (ἁγιασμός), sanctification, is used of (*a*) separation to God, 1 Cor. 1 : 30 ; 2 Thess. 2 : 13 ; 1 Pet. 1 : 2 ; (*b*) the course of life befitting those so separated, 1 Thess. 4 : 3, 4, 7 ; Rom. 6 : 19, 22 ; 1 Tim. 2 : 15 ; Heb. 12 : 14.¶ " Sanctification is that relationship with God into which men enter by faith in Christ, Acts 26 : 18 ; 1 Cor. 6 : 11, and to which their sole title is the death of Christ, Eph. 5 : 25, 26 ; Col. 1 : 22 ; Heb. 10 : 10, 29 ; 13 : 12.

" Sanctification is also used in N.T. of the separation of the believer from evil things and ways. This sanctification is God's will for the believer, 1 Thess. 4 : 3, and His purpose in calling him by the gospel, ver. 7 ; it must be learned from God, ver. 4, as He teaches it by His Word, John 17 : 17, 19 ; cp. Ps. 17 : 4 ; 119 : 9, and it must be pursued by the believer, earnestly and undeviatingly, 1 Tim. 2 : 15 ; Heb. 12 : 14. For the holy character, *hagiōsunē*, 1 Thess. 3 : 13, is not vicarious, i.e., it cannot be transferred or imputed, it is an individual possession, built up, little by little, as the result of obedience to the Word of God, and of following the example of Christ, Matt. 11 : 29 ; John 13 : 15 ; Eph. 4 : 20 ; Phil. 2 : 5, in the power of the Holy Spirit, Rom. 8 : 13 ; Eph. 3 : 16.

" The Holy Spirit is the Agent in sanctification, Rom. 15 : 16 ; 2 Thess. 2 : 13 ; 1 Pet. 1 : 2 ; cp. 1 Cor. 6 : 11. . . . The sanctification of the Spirit is associated with the choice, or election, of God ; it is a Divine

SAN	318	SAN

act preceding the acceptance of the Gospel by the individual."*
For synonymous words see HOLINESS.

B. Verb.

HAGIAZŌ (ἁγιάζω), to sanctify, " is used of (*a*) the gold adorning the Temple and of the gift laid on the altar, Matt. 23 : 17, 19 ; (*b*) food, 1 Tim. 4 : 5 ; (*c*) the unbelieving spouse of a believer, 1 Cor. 7 : 14 ; (*d*) the ceremonial cleansing of the Israelites, Heb. 9 : 13 ; (*e*) the Father's Name, Luke 11 : 2 ; (*f*) the consecration of the Son by the Father, John 10 : 36 ; (*g*) the Lord Jesus devoting Himself to the redemption of His people, John 17 : 19 ; (*h*) the setting apart of the believer for God, Acts 20 : 32 ; cp. Rom. 15 : 16 ; (*i*) the effect on the believer of the Death of Christ, Heb. 10 : 10, said of God, and 2 : 11 ; 13 : 12, said of the Lord Jesus ; (*j*) the separation of the believer from the world in his behaviour— by the Father through the Word, John 17 : 17, 19 ; (*k*) the believer who turns away from such things as dishonour God and His gospel, 2 Tim. 2 : 21 ; (*l*) the acknowledgment of the Lordship of Christ, 1 Pet. 3 : 15.

" Since every believer is sanctified in Christ Jesus, 1 Cor. 1 : 2, cp.

Zondervan's Pictorial Bible Dictionary

office of Israel's first two kings.   C.E.D.

SANBALLAT (săn-bălʹăt, Heb. *sanvallat*, Assyr. *Sin-uballit, the god Sin has given life*), a Horonite; that is, a man of Beth-horon. He was a very influential Samaritan who tried unsuccessfully to defeat Nehemiah's plans for rebuilding the walls of Jerusalem (Neh. 4:1ff). He then plotted with others to invite Nehemiah to a conference at Ono in order to assassinate him, but Nehemiah saw through his stratagem and refused to come. When this device failed, he tried vainly to intimidate the Jewish governor (Neh. 6:5-14). Sanballat's daughter married into the family of Eliashib, the high priest at the time of the annulment of the mixed marriages forbidden by the Law (Neh. 13:28), but her husband refused to forsake her, and went with her to Shechem, where he became the high priest of a new temple built by his father-in-law on Gerizim. Sanballat's name is mentioned in some interesting papyri letters found at the end of the 19th century in Egypt. He was then the governor of Samaria.

SANCTIFICATION (sănk-tĭ-fĭ-kăʹshŭn, Gr. *hagiasmós*, a *separation, setting apart*). While the noun does not occur in the OT, the verb "to sanctify" (Heb. *qādhash*), appears frequently. Its meaning is not primarily ethical but formal, its fundamental force being to separate from the world and consecrate to God. To sanctify anything is to declare that it belongs to God. It may refer to persons, places, days and seasons, and objects used for worship. Among objects sanctified to Jehovah in the OT are the first-born of Israel (Exod. 13:2), the Levites (Num. 3:12), the priests and the tent of meeting (Exod. 29:44), the altar (Exod. 29: 36), the offering (Exod. 29:27), the Sabbath (Neh. 13:19-22), the nation of Israel as a whole (Exod. 19:5,6), a man's house or his field (Lev. 27:14, 16). To sanctify Jehovah means to put Him in a category by Himself, to acknowledge Him as God, to recognize Him as supreme, sovereign, with a unique claim on all of His creation. When Christ sanctifies Himself (John 17:19), He means that He consecrates Himself to His mediatorial work, as Redeemer. The word "saint" comes from the same root and means "a sanctified one" — one who belongs to Christ. This formal meaning appears in I Corinthians 7:12-14, where the unbelieving husband is said to be sanctified by the wife, meaning not that he is different in moral character, but stands in a certain privileged relation to God.

In an ethical sense sanctification means the progressive conformation of the believer into the image of Christ, or the process by which the life is made morally holy. The transformation of the believer's life and character follows naturally from his consecration to a God who is morally perfect. Now that we belong to Christ we are to live to Him (Eph. 4:1; Col. 3:1-4; I Thess. 5:10). God has made a twofold provision for the believer's sanctification: the redemptive work of Christ and the work of the indwelling Holy Spirit. Sanctification has its beginning when a person becomes a Christian. God then, in regeneration, implants a new life in man, and gives to him the Holy Spirit, who makes real in his experience that for which Christ died for him at Calvary. It is in Romans 6-8 that we have the most extended teaching in the Bible on the ground and experimental outworking of sanctification. In a sense it is a gift, as is every part of salvation, but it must be daily appropriated through the moral surrender of our life to God. It is not momentary and instantaneous, but a life-long process, completed only when we see Christ. See HOLINESS.   S.B.

SANCTUARY (săngkʹtū-â-rē, Heb. *miqdāsh*, Gr. *hágion, holy place*), refers almost exclusively to the tabernacle or temple. God's sanctuary was His established earthly abode, the place where He chose to dwell among His people. Psalm 114:2 says that "Judah was his sanctuary, and Israel his dominion." God Himself is a sanctuary for His people (Isa. 8:14; Ezek. 11:19). The word is used particularly of the holy of holies, whether of the tabernacle or temple. When it is used in the plural, it usually denotes idolatrous shrines, or high places, which Israelites who compromised with heathenism sometimes built (Amos 7:9). A sanctuary was also a place of asylum, the horns of the altar especially being regarded as inviolable (cf. I Kings 2: 28f). In the NT the word is used only in the Epistle to the Hebrews (8:2; 9:1,2; 13:11), where the author makes clear that the earthly sanctuary was only a type of the true sanctuary which is in heaven, of which Christ is the high priest, and in which He offers Himself as a sacrifice (Heb. 10: 1-18).   S.B.

Hendriksen's Commentary on 1 Thessalonians

4:3-8   I THESSALONIANS

3-8. Because of the exegetical problem involved in verses 3-8, and in order to show the relationship of the several parts to each other and to the whole, it was necessary to print these six verses together as one unit, and to print them in such a manner that these relationships are at once apparent.

For this is God's will, y o u r sanctification,

(a) that y o u abstain from immorality,

(b) that each one of y o u know how to take a wife for himself in sanctification and honor, not in the passion of lust like also the heathen who do not know God;

(c) that (no one) go beyond what is proper and defraud his brother in this matter,

because an Avenger is the Lord in all these things, as previously we told y o u, and solemnly testified. For God did not call us for uncleanness but in sanctification. Therefore, he who rejects (this instruction), rejects not man but God who even gives his Holy Spirit to y o u.

Thus, it becomes apparent at once that, according to the most simple construction (also the most logical, it seems to us), the words *This . . . God's will . . . y o u r sanctification* are in apposition. The three co-ordinate clauses (a, b, and c) are added for further elucidation (in other words, they are *epexegetical*) of the concept *y o u r sanctification*. (See also on verse 9.) They are in apposition with it and give it a somewhat restricted application.   Also (b) sheds light on (a), (a) on (b), (c) on (b), and (b) on (c). Though (b) and (c) are parallel to each other and in a sense also to (a), yet they may be viewed as presenting a specific exemplification of (a).

The clause "because an Avenger is the Lord in all these things . . ." modifies (a), (b), and (c), as the very words *all these things* indicate. The sense of that clause is: God avenges immorality, and in particular the taking of a wife in the passion of lust, and the evil of going beyond what is proper and defrauding the brother in the matter of marital relationships. God punishes the man who refuses to tread the path of sanctification. This is true, "*for* God did not call us for uncleanness but in sanctification." The final sentence — "Therefore, he who rejects (this instruction) rejects not man but God who even gives his Holy Spirit to y o u" — shows that because it was God himself who called in connection with sanctification, the man who disregards this admonition squarely opposes *him* (see N.T.C. on John 13:20; cf. I Sam. 8:7; Luke 10:16), and that this is all the more reprehensible because the Author of sanctification is God's great *gift* to the Church.

From the preceding it is clear that Paul is discussing *one* matter, not *two*. He is discussing *sanctification*, and here in verses 3-8 in particular the duty of everyone to abstain from *immorality*, such as is practiced, for

Lesson 18

INTERPRETATION - WHAT DOES IT MEAN?
Basic Helps Practice

Please read 1 Thessalonians and write down any words, ideas or verses you would like to research. Do as much as you can before class and record your findings. In class we will share our discoveries and research other areas of interest.

_____

_____

_____

_____

_____

_____

_____

_____

_____

_____

_____

_____

_____

_____

_____

_____

_____

Objective:

To practice using some of the basic tools of Bible study.

APPLICATION - WHAT DOES IT MEAN TO ME?

How to Apply? - Part 1

Notice the progression in the "seeing" in John 20:4-8. In vs. 5, John "saw" (*blepei* meaning, "a mere viewing of facts from without," *Vines*). In vs. 6, Peter "saw" (*theorei* meaning, "to view attentively... stresses more especially the action of the person beholding," *Vines*). In vs. 8, John "saw" (*eiden* meaning, "it especially indicates the direction of the thought to the object seen," *Vines*).

First, there was the *viewing* of the facts, then the attentive look, then a perception of the *meaning* of the facts. Note the result in vs. 8—"believed." They made the *application*.

Objective:

The purpose of this lesson is to help us understand how to move to the application of the text in our lives.

I.   **Application**

Application of a passage must be based on diligent observation of what the passage is saying and accurate interpretation of what the passage means.

A.   There has been a shift in the religious world to the "devotional" approach to Bible study. Sometimes this approach asks, "What does it say to my heart?" without first understanding what the passage says or means.

1.   This has led to a very superficial understanding of the Bible and misapplication of many texts.

B.   On the other hand, it is possible to treat Bible study as a dry, academic exercise with no application to our personal lives.

1.   This will lead to an understanding of the text but no transformation of life.

C. God makes a clear connection between understanding His word and application to our lives.

    1. How did Jesus describe the man who both "hears" and "does" in Matthew 7:24-27? _____

       _____

       _____

D. The authority of the Scriptures demands that we make application.

    1. How did the Thessalonians accept the teaching of Paul and why is this significant (1 Thessalonians 2:13)? _____

       _____

       _____

       _____

E. Scriptures have a goal.

    1. What profit can the scriptures have in our lives (2 Timothy 3:16-17)? _____

       _____

       _____

       _____

II.   Prayer

Prayer is the constant companion of Bible study. We should pray to God for help and guidance in applying any passage.

A. For what did Paul pray in Colossians 1:9-10? _____

    _____

    _____

    _____

III. Questions

Questions will help us apply the truths of God to our lives. Read 1 Thessalonians 1-2 and read through these questions with that text in mind. We will discuss what you have found in class.

A. How would the *original readers* have applied this passage?

    1. What is parallel about our life's situation?

    2. What are the cultural differences between us?

       a. The truth of God is valid in any culture, but not all culture recorded in the Bible reflects God's truth.

      (1) For example, many in the Old Testament fathered children by concubines and multiple wives.

      (2) What other examples can you think of? _____

_____

_____

_____

  b. Truths of God may find different applications in different cultures.

      (1) For example, the slave/master instruction is applicable today in the employee/employer relationship.

      (2) What other examples can you think of? _____

_____

_____

_____

  3. What time (dispensational) differences are there?

    a. For example, the Law of Moses would apply to us differently than to the Old Testament Jewish to whom it was given.

B. Is there a *statement* of God's will or *command* to be followed?

  1. Is it general or specific in its application?

    a. General commands give us the liberty to apply according to wise judgment.

      (1) List an example (from 1 Thessalonians if possible)

_____

_____

    b. Specific commands give us no liberty to deviate in any way.

      (1) List an example (from 1 Thessalonians if possible)

_____

_____

  2. We are more likely to find these statements/commands that apply to us in the *teaching portions* of the Gospels, Acts and NT letters.

  3. Self exam—Am I following these commands/statements? Is there an area of my life I need to change?

APPLICATION - WHAT DOES IT MEAN TO ME?
How to Apply? - Part 2

III. Questions (continued from previous lesson)

C. Is there an *example* of the people of God acting in a way that is *approved* of by God? We are to be imitators of NT Christians who were following the Lord's will.

1. List an example (from 1 Thessalonians if possible)_____

    _____

    _____

    _____

2. It is important to determine whether it is to be part of the pattern God wants us to follow. There are some questions which help to clarify.

    a. Where is the approval or disapproval of God found in the text?

    b. Is it consistent throughout all other examples?

    c. What command or principle of God does it reflect?

    d. What is the significance of the practice?

3. For the most part, approved examples will be found in the *historical writing*, such as recorded concerning Jesus' life, the disciples lives in the book of Acts, the NT letters and/or Revelation.

Objective:

The purpose of this lesson is to help us understand how to move to the application of the text in our lives.

    4. Self exam—Am I following in these God-approved footsteps? Is there an area of my life I need to change?

D. Is there something in the text which is not stated but *inferred*?

    1. List an example (from 1 Thessalonians if possible) _____

       _____

       _____

       _____

    2. Many inferences can be made from any passage. For an inference to be binding, however, it must be *necessarily inferred*. This means the text would not be complete without that inference.

    3. Self exam—Am I following this teaching? Is there an area of my life I need to change?

E. What *belief* does God want me to accept or reject from this passage?

    1. What belief about myself?

    2. What belief about God?

    3. What belief about others?

    4. What belief about my eternal destiny?

    5. List a belief you find in 1 Thessalonians_____

       _____

       _____

    6. Self exam—What beliefs do I already hold and how are they in harmony with or different from God's standard?

F. What *attitude* does God want me to take on or avoid?

    1. What attitude is being exemplified or taught?

    2. What attitude do I have?

    3. List an attitude found in 1 Thessalonians_____

       _____

    4. Self exam—What changes do I need to make to bring my attitudes in harmony with God's standard?

    5. What in the text help me know how to make the changes I need?

G. What action does God want me to *do* or *not do*?

    1. What action is being exemplified or taught?

    2. List an action you find in 1 Thessalonians _____

    _____

    3. Self exam—What is my behavior in these areas and how is it in harmony with or different from the standard of God?

H. What *promise* can I claim?

    1. Is the promise of the passage related only to the individuals discussed, or is the application broader to include me?

    2. Are there conditions placed on the promise?

    3. List a promise you find in 1 Thessalonians_____

    _____

    3. Self exam—Do I embrace this promise? Do I believe it? Why or why not?

Observation, **interpretation** and **application** lead to ***transformation***.

I beseech you therefore, brethren, by the mercies of God, that you present your bodies a **living sacrifice**, holy, acceptable to God, which is your **reasonable service**.

And do not be conformed to this world, but be **transformed** by the renewing of your mind, that you may prove what is the **good** and **acceptable** and **perfect will** of God.

- Romans 12:1-2

APPLICATION - WHAT DOES IT MEAN TO ME?
1 Thessalonians 1

Please read and study 1 Thessalonians 1 and make application to your own life following the principles of observation, interpretation and application. In particular, prayerfully answer the questions found in lessons 19 and 20. Record your observations and answers on this and the following page.

_____

_____

_____

_____

_____

_____

_____

_____

_____

_____

_____

_____

_____

_____

_____

_____

Objective:

The purpose of this lesson is to make the application of the text in our lives.

APPLICATION - WHAT DOES IT MEAN TO ME?
1 Thessalonians 2 and 3

Please read and study 1 Thessalonians 2 and 3 and make application to your own life following the principles of observation, interpretation and application. In particular, prayerfully answer the questions found in lessons 19 and 20. Record your observations and answers on this and the following page.

_____

_____

_____

_____

_____

_____

_____

_____

_____

_____

_____

_____

_____

_____

_____

_____

Objective:

The purpose of this lesson is to make the application of the text in our lives.

APPLICATION - WHAT DOES IT MEAN TO ME?
1 Thessalonians 4:1-12

Please read and study 1 Thessalonians 4:1-12 and make application to your own life following the principles of observation, interpretation and application. In particular, prayerfully answer the questions found in lessons 19 and 20. Record your observations and answers on this and the following page.

_____

_____

_____

_____

_____

_____

_____

_____

_____

_____

_____

_____

_____

_____

_____

_____

_____

Objective:

The purpose of this lesson is to make the application of the text in our lives.

Lesson 24

APPLICATION - WHAT DOES IT MEAN TO ME?
1 Thessalonians 4:13-5:11

Please read and study 1 Thessalonians 4:13-5:11 and make application to your own life following the principles of observation, interpretation and application. In particular, prayerfully answer the questions found in lessons 19 and 20. Record your observations and answers on this and the following page.

_____

_____

_____

_____

_____

_____

_____

_____

_____

_____

_____

_____

_____

_____

_____

_____

_____

Objective:

The purpose of this lesson is to make the application of the text in our lives.

APPLICATION - WHAT DOES IT MEAN TO ME?
1 Thessalonians 5:12-28

Please read and study 1 Thessalonians 5:12-28 and make application to your own life following the principles of observation, interpretation and application. In particular, prayerfully answer the questions found in lessons 19 and 20. Record your observations and answers on this and the following page.

_____

_____

_____

_____

_____

_____

Objective:

The purpose of this lesson is to make the application of the text in our lives.

_____

_____

_____

_____

_____

_____